Depth Study

The Rise and Fall of the British Empire

Aaron Wilkes

Author's acknowledgements

The author wishes to thank Kate Redmond for all her hard work, good humour and advice. He would also like to thank Emma, Hannah and Eleanor Wilkes for all their support, patience and encouragement during the preparation of this book.

© 2010 Folens Limited, on behalf of the author.

United Kingdom: Folens Publishers, Waterslade House, Thame Road, Haddenham, Buckinghamshire, HP17 8NT.

Email: folens@folens.com   Website: www.folens.com

Ireland: Folens Publishers, Greenhills Road, Tallaght, Dublin 24.

Email: info@folens.ie   Website: www.folens.ie

Editor: Kate Redmond
Text design and layout: Sally Boothroyd
Picture researcher: Sue Sharp
Illustrators: Tony Randell and Clive Wakfer
Cover design: Anthony Finch and Rosa Capacchione
Cover images: © iStockphoto.com/nicoolay (left);
© INTERFOTO/Alamy (centre); © North Wind Picture Archives/Alamy (right)

The websites recommended in this publication were correct at the time of going to press; however, websites may have been removed or web addresses changed since that time. Folens has made every attempt to suggest websites that are reliable and appropriate for students' use. It is not unknown for unscrupulous individuals to put unsuitable material on websites that may be accessed by students. Teachers should check all websites before allowing students to access them. Folens is not responsible for the content of external websites.

For general spellings Folens adheres to the *Oxford Dictionary of English*, Second Edition (Revised), 2005.

First published 2010 by Folens Limited.

British Library Cataloguing in Publication Data. A catalogue record for this publication is available from the British Library.

ISBN 978-1-85008-550-8   Folens code   FD5508

Acknowledgements

Topfoto/Granger Collection, New York: 8, 9 (top right), 21 (left), 41; Topfoto: 9 (bottom left); The Gallery Collection/Corbis: 10; www.heritage-history.com: 12; The Granger Collection New York/Topfoto: 13; MPI/Getty Images: 14; Employments for Gentlemen, plate XI, from 'America, Part X', Latin edition, 1619 (engraving), Bry, Theodore de (1528–98)/Virginia Historical Society, Richmond, Virginia, USA/The Bridgeman Art Library: 15; Interfoto/AAA Collection: 19 (top left); Time Life Pictures/War Department/National Archives/Getty Images: 19 (centre); The Art Gallery Collection/Alamy: 20, 74 (top left); Lebrecht Music and Arts Photo Library/Alamy: 21 (top right); English Heritage Photo Library: 22 (top right); Jeff Greenberg/Alamy: 22 (bottom left); akg-images/British Library: 23 (top right); Pictorial Press Ltd/Alamy: 23 (bottom); Copyright 2010 photolibrary.com: 26 (bottom left), 26 (bottom right); iStockphoto: 27 (top left), 27 (right), 34 (bottom right), 44 (top right); INTERFOTO/Alamy: 27 (bottom left), 67; British Library/HIP/TopFoto: 28, 32 (bottom); Mary Evans Picture Library: 29, 34 (top left), 35 (right), 36, 37 (both), 43 (left), 47, 48 (bottom left), 50, 51, 54, 59, 60 (top), 68, 80; The 7th Bengal Infantry on Parade, the Anglo-Indian Army of the 1880s (colour litho), Simkin, Richard (1840–1926) (after)/Private Collection/Peter Newark Pictures/The Bridgeman Art Library: 30; The Art Archive/Alamy: 31; Bettmann/CORBIS: 32 (top), 38; Hulton-Deutsch Collection/CORBIS: 35 (left); Topical Press Agency/Getty Images: 39; Adrian Pingstone, Public Domain: 43 (right); Illustrated London News Ltd/Mary Evans: 44 (bottom left), 69; London Stereoscopic Company/Getty Images: 44 (bottom right); Steffen Hauser/botanikfoto/Alamy: 46; Mary Evans Picture Library/Alamy: 48 (top right); PA/EMPICS: 53; Nick Wilson/ALLSPORT/Getty Images: 55; The Signing of the Treaty of Waitangi by Captain Hobson and the Maori chiefs in 1840, 1938 (oil on canvas) by King, Marcus (20th century) Alexander Turnbull Library, Wellington, New Zealand/The Bridgeman Art Library: 58 (top right); Merrett, Joseph Jenner, 1816–1854. War dance, New Zealand [ca. 1845] 1 watercolour; 19.2 x 30.3 cm, National Library of Australia: 58 (bottom left); Alexander Turnbull Library, New Zealand: 60 (bottom); Mary Evans Picture Library 2010: 61; Mirrorpix: 62 (left); Ministry of Defence: 62 (centre); Swim Ink 2, LLC/CORBIS: 62 (bottom right); Niday Picture Library/Alamy: 63 (top); Imperial War Museum: 63 (bottom); Public Domain: 64; Australian War Memorial Negative Number 044167: 65 (top); HIP/ Imagestate: 65 (bottom); The Defence of Rorke's Drift, 1880 (oil on canvas) by Neuville, Alphonse Marie de (1835–85) Art Gallery of New South Wales, Sydney, Australia/The Bridgeman Art Library: 73; akg-images: 74 (bottom right); City of London, London Metropolitan Archives: 75; Harry Benson/Getty Images): 77 (top left); LUIS ENRIQUE ASCUI/Reuters/Corbis: 77 (top right); Comic Relief: 77 (bottom); Peter Evans/Alamy: 78; ros images – Fotolia.com: 79 (top left); United Archives GmbH/Alamy: 79 (top right); PA Archive/Press Association Images: 79 (centre left), 79 (centre right); Corbis: 79 (bottom); RUSSELL BOYCE/Reuters/Corbis: 80 (top).

'A True Relation of Occurrences and Accidents in Virginia, 1608', John Smith, in 'Travels and Works of Captain John Smith, President of Virginia, and Admiral of New England, 1580–1631, Part I', John Smith (ed. Edward Arber), John Grant, 1910: 14; Nova Britannia, R.I., The Virginia Company, 1609: 15; 'The Indian Freedom Struggle', http://india.gov.in, 2008: 33; William Dalrymple, in a BBC interview by Soutik Biswas, BBC News website, September 2006: 33; 'Pax Britannica', James Morris, 1968, cited in 'Expansion, Trade and Industry', Ros Adams, Causeway Press Ltd., 1992: 34, 40; 'Indian Home Rule', Mohandas K. Gandhi, Navajivan Publishing, 1938 (reprinted in 1946): 35; 'The English in India: A Problem of Politics', J.A.R. Marriott, Clarendon Press, 1932: 36; Based on poster from Bridgeman Art Library/Wilberforce House, Hull City Museums and Art Galleries, UK: 41; 'The Endeavour Journal', James Cook, April 1770: 48; 'Christianity the Means of Civilisation: The evidence given before a Committee of the House of Commons on Aborigines', Seeley and Burnside, 1835: 54; 'The Oxford History of the British Empire: The twentieth century', Judith Brown and William Roger Louis, Oxford University Press, 1999: 63; 'The Oxford Companion to World War II', L.C.B. Dear and M.R.D. Foot, Oxford University Press, 2001: 65; 'Expansion, Trade and Industry', Ros Adams, Causeway Press Ltd., 1992: 67; 'Zulu: The true story', Dr Saul David, BBC History in-depth, 2009: 73

Contents

What is history? 4

INTRODUCTION:
What is an empire? 6

BIG QUESTION:
How did the British Empire begin? 8

BIG QUESTION:
How did the Empire grow? 10

DEPTH STUDY: BRITISH AMERICA 14
1: Jamestown 1607: Are you tough enough? 14
2: Life in the colonies 16
3: Was Britain involved in the slave trade? 18
4: Revolution 20

BIG QUESTION:
Should Britain make up for its role in slavery? 22

DEPTH STUDY: INDIA 26
1: India before the Brits 26
2: An Indian takeaway 28
3: Indian Mutiny… or a War of Independence? 30
4: 'The Jewel in the Crown' 34
5: Independence for India 36

Have you been learning? 1 40

BIG QUESTION:
So how big was the British Empire? 42

BIG QUESTION:
What did the Empire do for Britain? 44

DEPTH STUDY: A LAND DOWN UNDER 46
1: Finding Australia 46
2: Transportation nation 50
3: Adventure or invasion? 52
4: An independent Australia 56
5: What about New Zealand? 58

BIG QUESTION:
Did the Empire strike back? 60

BIG QUESTION:
Did the Empire help win two World Wars? 62

DEPTH STUDY: AFRICA 66
1: The scramble for Africa 66
2: Zulu 70
3: How did a war in Africa change British schools? 74
4: Independence in Africa 76

BIG QUESTION:
What is the legacy of the British Empire? 78

BIG QUESTION:
Was the British Empire a good or a bad thing? 82

Have you been learning? 2 84

Glossary 86
Index 87

MERCHISTON CASTLE
SCHOOL
HISTORY DEPARTMENT

What is history?

Before you start this book, take a few minutes to think about these questions.

- What do you think history is? What does the word mean?
- What have you learnt in history lessons before, perhaps in your primary school or in other years at secondary school? Did you enjoy them or not? If you enjoyed them, say why. If you didn't enjoy them, why not?
- Have you read any history books or stories about things that happened a long time ago? Have you watched any television programmes, films or plays about things that happened in the past? If so, which ones?

History is about what happened in the past. It is about people in the past, what they did and why they did it, what they thought and what they felt. To enjoy history you need to have a good imagination. You need to be able to imagine what life was like in the past, or what it may have been like to be involved in past events.

How did people feel, think and react to events like these?

The year is 1607 and we have just arrived in England's new settlement in the New World. We are certain that the land is good for growing crops, which we can sell back in Europe and make our fortunes. We might even find gold too! However, life isn't going to be easy out here. I hope we plant the right food… and avoid illness… and don't end up at war with the local native tribes who I know are in this area…

The invaders from Britain call this land 'Australia'… and they claim to own it! They are driving us off land that our ancestors have lived on for thousands of years. They say we are uncivilized… yet it is the British who send out their criminals to this land! Some of my fellow tribesmen are going to fight the British… but should I join them?

The 1930s will be a momentous decade in India's history. The British have dominated for years – but now the cry for Indian independence is louder than ever. Whilst it is difficult not to acknowledge some of the benefits of British rule, there is little doubt that Indians are now ready to rule themselves! But will the British allow India to become independent? If so, how will they achieve it? If not… what will Indians do about it?

How to use this book

As you work through this book, you will notice a number of features that keep appearing.

All sections of this book will start by setting your Mission Objectives. These are your key aims that set out your learning targets for the work ahead. Topics will end by trying to get you to assess your own learning. If you can accomplish each Mission Objective then you are doing well!

WISE-UP Words

WISE-UP Words are key terms that are vital to help you discuss and understand the topics. You can spot them easily because they are in bold type. Look up their meanings in a dictionary or use the Glossary at the end of the book. The Glossary is a list of words and their meanings.

PAUSE for Thought

Some topics contain PAUSE for Thought boxes. This is an opportunity for you to stop and think for yourself.

Hungry for MORE

The Hungry for MORE features give you a chance to extend your knowledge and research beyond the classroom. This is a time for you to take responsibility for your own learning. You might be asked to research something in the library or on the Internet, work on a presentation, or design and make something. Can you meet the challenge?

FACT

These are all the fascinating, amazing or astounding little bits of history that you usually don't get to hear about! But in Folens History we think they are just as important and give you insights into topics that you'll easily remember.

BIG QUESTION

This book asks you to consider some of the 'Big Questions' about the British Empire – these are the questions that challenge you to think hard about the most important issues facing the largest empire the world has ever seen.

There are also four Depth Studies in this book. These will get you to focus on the following themes:

- **BRITISH AMERICA**
- **INDIA**
- **A LAND DOWN UNDER**
- **AFRICA**

These Depth Studies focus on four key areas around the world where the British controlled huge areas of land.

Work sections are your opportunity to demonstrate your knowledge and understanding. You might be asked to put events in the correct chronological order. You might be asked to:

- explain how things have changed over time
- work out why two people might interpret the same event differently
- work out what triggered an event to take place in the short term or the long term.

What is an empire?

MISSION OBJECTIVES

- To understand what an 'empire' is – and identify some of the reasons why countries build empires.

Empires have existed for thousands and thousands of years. In schools and colleges today, the topic of 'empires' is taught often. In fact, many of you reading this now will have studied one or two empires – the Romans perhaps… or the Incas… or the Aztecs. The Egyptians even had a sort of empire too. So what exactly is an empire?

Empire explained

An empire is a collection of tribes, regions, territories, states or even countries that are ruled over and controlled by one leader or 'mother' country. The areas controlled by the 'mother country' are usually called **colonies**. However, they are sometimes called **protectorates**, **dominions** or **dependencies**. The mother country then makes many of the key decisions to do with the places it rules over.

So how does a country get an empire?

Force is the main method used by a country to build up an empire. To put it simply, a rich, powerful nation with plenty of soldiers and lots of weapons would find a 'weaker' territory or nation and just march in and take over. Sometimes deals were made with the weaker nations to avoid full-scale war – but, in general, it was the large, well-organized countries with big armies who were the 'empire-builders'. This was how one of the world's most famous empires – the Roman Empire – grew so large over 2000 years ago (see Source B).

! FACT **Why is it called that?** The word 'empire' comes from the Roman word 'imperium', which was a sort of legal title meaning that a person was in charge of something. For example, a person having 'imperium' in the army meant they had complete control.

↵ **SOURCE A:** *The Roman Army was a formidable fighting force. The Roman Empire expanded as a result of years of bitter warfare.*

SOURCE B: *The Romans built up their Empire gradually from about 31 BCE. It lasted over 400 years. Wars and battles with rival tribes and nations meant that the Roman Empire was constantly changing its boundaries, but this map shows the Empire at its maximum extent, around 130 CE.* ↘

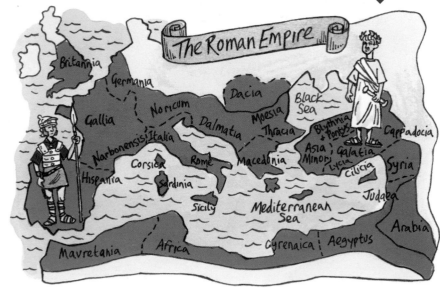

The Roman Empire

Why do countries want empires?

There are lots of reasons why some countries try to take over others. After a war, the winning nation may take over the defeated one and include it in their empire – as a sort of punishment for losing! Other countries go 'empire-hunting' because they want more resources like grain, cattle, gold, silver, tin or iron. They take over other countries in order to steal all the things they want. Sometimes countries have even taken over territory just to stop rival nations getting it first! On other occasions countries have invaded others because they thought they had a 'right' to the land, or felt that they were doing the natives a favour by teaching them a new way of life.

↳ **SOURCE C:** *In the 1500s, the Spanish Empire was one of the largest in the world. In fact, they conquered and took over two other empires – the Inca and Aztec Empires of South America... and took all their gold!*

The rise and fall of empires

Over many thousands of years there have been many different empires. There are some very famous ones – like the Roman, Inca and Aztec Empires – but lots of other civilizations and nations have had empires at one time or another too. The list includes the Egyptians, Persians, Greeks, French, Germans, Russians, Turks, Austrians, Chinese and Japanese. More often than not, each empire has ended because they have been defeated by a fresh, powerful, up-and-coming country, which takes its place as the world's most powerful 'empire nation'!

The largest empire in the world

One country not mentioned so far is Britain. But from small beginnings in the early 1600s, Britain's Empire grew and grew to be – quite simply – the largest empire the world had ever known. By 1900, land nearly 40 times the size of Britain itself belonged to the British Empire. Britain ruled over 450 million people living in 56 different places all over the world. This amounted to approximately one-quarter of the world's population and one-quarter of the Earth's total land area!

But 50 years later, after two World Wars, the British Empire began to break apart. More and more countries wanted nothing to do with Britain. They wanted a chance to run their countries themselves – they wanted their independence. And Britain was in no position to stop them. Indeed, the rise and fall of the British Empire is a truly remarkable story!

★ WISE-UP Words

colony
dependency   dominion
empire   protectorate

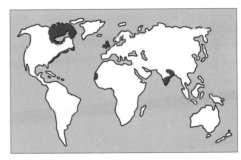

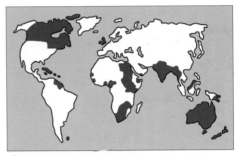

↳ **SOURCE D:** *The growth of the British Empire, 1750–1900.*

Work

1 a In your own words, explain what is meant by the terms 'empire' and 'colony'.

b Why do you think the term 'mother country' is sometimes used when describing empire nations?

c What was the main method nations used to build empires?

2 List three reasons why some countries built up empires.

3 a Write down the subtitle 'The British Empire' and then write down five facts about it.

b Look at Source D, particularly the lower map. Can you name any of the countries that were once part of the British Empire?

MISSION ACCOMPLISHED?

- Can you name five empire nations of the past?
- Can you explain (in no more than 20 words) what an empire is?

How did the British Empire begin?

MISSION OBJECTIVES

• To understand the importance of Henry VII and John Cabot in the story of the British Empire.

The British Empire began on 5 March 1496. On this very date the first Tudor King of England, Henry VII (Henry VIII's dad), asked an Italian explorer to go out and search the world for any 'islands, countries, regions or provinces' that were 'unknown to all Christians'. The explorer was instructed that, if he discovered any new lands, he was to claim them for England.

Believe it or not, King Henry's famous request laid the foundations for the start of the British Empire – the largest empire the world had ever known. So why did King Henry ask the explorer to set sail? Where did the explorer sail to? And what exactly did he find?

An age of discovery

In the late 1400s, Europeans were finding out more and more about their world. Across Europe, writers, sculptors, doctors, mathematicians, scientists, painters and designers started to realize that some of their current methods and ideas were wrong and there were better ways of doing things. They began to ask questions and experiment with new ideas. This period in history is often called the 'Renaissance', which is an Italian word for 'rebirth'. It got its name because many people thought the experience of learning new things was like being 'reborn'.

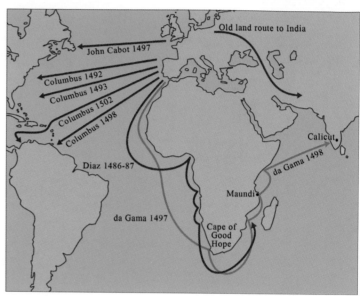

↰ SOURCE B: *A modern map showing the routes taken by explorers, 1486–1502:*
- *Bartholomew Diaz (from Portugal), 1486–1487.*
- *Christopher Columbus (Italian for Spain), 1492–1502.*
- *John Cabot (Italian for England), 1497.*
- *Vasco da Gama (from Portugal), 1498.*

↰ SOURCE A: *A map of the world, created in 1489. This is the full extent of what the Europeans knew about the world at that time.*

Spain and Portugal

The Renaissance wasn't only a time when people were curious to know how the world worked – they were also keen to explore it and see what they could find. In the late 1400s, Spain and Portugal were two of the most powerful countries in Europe – and they both began to set up great world empires. Their kings were keen to find new lands to call their own, whilst Portuguese and Spanish merchants were eager to expand their businesses and find new sea routes to the Far East. In 1487, Portuguese ships became the first in Europe to get round the bottom of Africa. This opened up a sea route to India and the Far East… and the Portuguese made a fortune!

The Americas are discovered

Spain soon followed Portugal's example and in 1492 Spanish ships under the guidance of Christopher Columbus (an Italian working for Spain) set out for China, but headed in the opposite direction – westwards. Columbus knew that the world was round, and thought that to get to the East it was possible to sail west over the sea until you reached China and the Spice Islands. He was wrong – he didn't know the vast continents of America would get in his way!

After reaching this unexpected new land, Columbus claimed much of South America and the Caribbean for Spain. Soon Portugal claimed Brazil. But neither Spain nor Portugal landed in North America (what we now call the USA and Canada), and it remained unexplored.

Here comes Henry

In 1496 England finally joined the age of exploration, when King Henry VII gave an Italian explorer called John Cabot the mission of finding new lands for England (see Source D). In 1497 Cabot sailed westwards from Bristol across the Atlantic Ocean. A few months later he landed on the coast of Newfoundland, in what we now call Canada (see Source B).

However, there were no silks, spices or gold to be found there – so Cabot came home! But this brief visit was the start of the British Empire. Over time, English settlers would move out to live in Canada – and more settlers would follow all along the North American coast. The age of British people taking land and living in overseas colonies had arrived!

SOURCE E:
A painting of John Cabot. His son Sebastian is also shown. ↱

! FACT Where in the world?

If you were a European in 1490, you would know the world was a round sphere (people hadn't thought it was flat for ages) but you wouldn't have a clue that the Americas, Australia or New Zealand existed. They did of course, and people lived there, but Europeans just hadn't found them yet!

! FACT American Indians

When Columbus arrived in the Caribbean he thought he'd found the East Indies – another name for the islands to the east of India. As a result, he called the tribesmen he met here 'Indians',.. and the name stuck! The area where he landed was even named the West Indies... and that name stuck too!

↵ **SOURCE C:** *Columbus had no idea he'd found a continent – he just thought he'd found new islands near to China and the Spice Islands that Europeans hadn't seen before. Only in later years, after explorers had found more and more of the 'Americas', did people realize that Columbus had been the first to find the 'New World'.*

'You have full and free authority to sail to all parts and countries of the East, West, and North under our banners and ensigns [flags] with five ships and as many sailors as they can hold, to seek out, discover and find whatever islands, countries, regions or provinces of the heathen and infidels whosoever they be, and in what part of the world they be, which before this time have been unknown to all Christians.'

↰ **SOURCE D:** *Orders given to John Cabot by Henry VII, March 1496. Find out what 'heathens' and 'infidels' are.*

Work

1 a What was the 'Renaissance'?
   b Can you think of two reasons why people at this time were keen to find new lands?

2 a Look at Source A. Describe the source – what does it show?
   b Which major continents were undiscovered by Europeans at the time this map was drawn?

3 a Explain what is meant by the word 'significant'.
   b How were Columbus, King Henry VII and Cabot 'significant' in the creation of the British Empire?

——MISSION ACCOMPLISHED?——

• Could you write a sentence or two explaining the importance of King Henry VII of England and John Cabot in the early years of the British Empire?

How did the Empire grow?

MISSION OBJECTIVES

- To understand why America became the first part of the British Empire.

Look at Source A. You should recognize the queen (it's Elizabeth I!), but if you look carefully you can see lots of other details too. In the background to the right you can see stormy weather and lots of wrecked Spanish ships. To the left you can see English ships sailing in the sunshine. This portrait was painted to commemorate England's defeat of the Spanish Navy (or Armada) in 1588. However, there is another fascinating part of the picture.

Notice the globe in the painting – the Queen is pointing to the newly found continent of the Americas, and particularly a region in North America called Virginia, which one of her explorers had claimed for her in 1588. He even named this new **colony** after her (as Elizabeth was known as 'The Virgin Queen'!). In fact at the time this painting was completed the first English child had just been born in Elizabeth's newest colony, and the baby was called… Virginia!

- So how exactly did Elizabeth get this land?
- Who got it for her?
- How did Elizabeth's new colony bring England into conflict with other countries?

A false start?

It was during the time of Queen Elizabeth's grandfather, King Henry VII, that Christopher Columbus was the first European to discover the Americas in 1492. He was followed by both Spain and their allies, Portugal, who were busy capturing and colonizing lots of land in South America, Central America and the Caribbean. They didn't pay much attention to what we now call the USA and Canada, because they thought this part of the continent needed too much work to make any money from it. It was much easier to get gold and silver from Mexico and South America instead.

The English, then, were left to claim land in North America and in 1497 John Cabot (an Italian working for Henry VII) claimed a huge area of Canada for the King. He called it Newfoundland, and it became the first part of England's new Empire.

↰ SOURCE A: *The Armada portrait, painted by George Gower in 1588.*

However, Cabot and his crew did not stay long. No English settlers went to live there and the native people continued to live their lives as they had done for thousands of years. Over the next few years Spanish, Portuguese, French and English fishermen went to catch cod in the area, but no one actually settled there!

In fact the kings and queens who immediately followed Henry VII (his son Henry VIII and then Edward VI and Mary I) did little to expand England's Empire. They were clearly proud of the land they had 'found' in the 'New World', but didn't send people to live over there. Instead they encouraged their explorers to find new trade routes to China, India and the Spice Islands.

But all this changed when Elizabeth I (Henry VII's granddaughter) became queen!

Look through the following story carefully – it shows how England's Empire grew and grew during Elizabeth I's reign.

By the mid 1500s Spain controlled lots of land in the Americas, including Cuba, Jamaica and Peru.

Whilst Spain could boast of finding gold, tobacco, potatoes, tomatoes, cotton, sugar and rum in their new colonies, England had to be content with sailing to the northern part of North America... and finding cod.

With Spain and Portugal controlling most of the trade routes to Central and South America, England's explorers had to find new ways to reach China, India and the Spice Islands by going above Russia and what we now call Canada.

Explorers like Hugh Willoughby, Richard Chancellor, Martin Frobisher and John Davis didn't find any new routes to China or India... but became sailing heroes because of their brave and exciting voyages.

Elizabeth even encouraged explorers like Sir Francis Drake, Sir Humphrey Gilbert and Sir John Hawkins to steal gold and silver from Spanish ships that were bringing it back to Spain from the New World. They also stole valuable maps and sea charts.

These men were known as **privateers** but really they were acting like pirates – with Queen Elizabeth's permission!

Elizabeth, who became Queen of England in 1559, quickly saw advantages in allowing her sailors to explore as much of the world as they could.

If they found new routes to faraway places, England would become wealthy through trade.

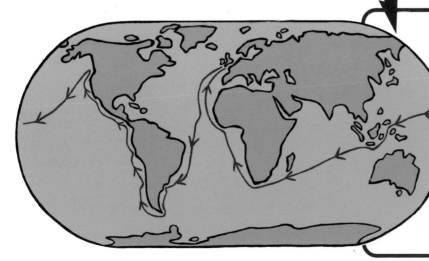

In 1577, the privateer Sir Francis Drake set off on a successful journey around the world. He became only the second man to do this. (The first was Portuguese explorer Ferdinand Magellan.)

On his way he landed on the western coast of America – and claimed it for England. He also stole more Spanish gold. From one ship he stole 40kg of gold, jewels, precious plates and 26 tons of silver. It could be worth about £12 million today!

In 1583 Sir Humphrey Gilbert was given permission by Queen Elizabeth to travel to Newfoundland (Canada) and set up a colony over there.

Gilbert claimed hundreds of miles of land for England – but the settlers gave up and came home. However, today the area around where Gilbert landed is regarded as the first part of the British Empire!

SOURCE B: ↳
A painting of Sir Humphrey Gilbert cutting the soil in Newfoundland in August 1583. This ceremony symbolized that the land around there was now English. The natives (see picture) had no say in the matter! The colony didn't last long and the settlers left after a few weeks – Gilbert himself was killed on the journey home when his ship sank in a storm!

In 1584 Queen Elizabeth sent one of her favourites, Sir Walter Raleigh, to start another settlement further down the coast from Gilbert's failed colony.

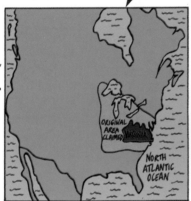

The new colony was named Virginia after a name Elizabeth was known by – 'The Virgin Queen'. The area of land Raleigh claimed was huge, covering hundreds of miles of North American coastline.

Raleigh didn't stay in Virginia but nearly 100 settlers (or colonists) tried to start new lives in this new English colony. Their settlement was called Roanoke.

However, the settlers were short on supplies, had little idea how to farm the land properly... and the local tribes were hostile.

When, after a few years, Raleigh tried to start another settlement in Virginia, all the new settlers found were empty cabins... and bones!

A friendly local tribe reported that the settlers had been attacked and those that survived had sailed up the coast in their boat... never to be seen again!

There were 117 settlers in the second group. They landed in July 1587.

On 18 August a woman named Eleanor Dare gave birth to the first English child born in America. She was named Virginia.

However, the settlers again struggled to survive and ran into difficulties with the local tribes.

In fact, the settlers found life so hard in the new colony that one of them, John White, returned to England to get fresh supplies and tools and to ask for help.

When White returned to the colony in 1590 he found it had been deserted. There was no sign of the men, women or children (including Virginia) and no sign of any fight or struggle.

The only clue was the word 'Croatoan' carved into a post and 'Cro' carved into a tree! The Croatan were a local tribe that had been friendly with the settlers.

WISE-UP Words

colony   East India Company
Moscow Company   privateers

None of the settlers were ever found and to this day, no one knows whether they ran away, or were killed by hostile tribes or even Spanish invaders.

Roanoke is often called 'The Lost Colony'... and it was several years before any more English colonists tried to settle in Virginia!

! FACT Names, names, names

European settlers in America called the local people 'Indians' (because the first explorers there thought they had landed in India!) or 'Redskins'. Today, they are known as Native Americans, Amerindians or First Americans.

⬑ **SOURCE C:** *Landing at Roanoke.*

Coming to America

The first few Virginian colonies and Newfoundland were failures – but without doubt, England had laid claim to a large part of the eastern coast of North America. As far as the English were concerned, this part of the New World belonged to them and they were prepared to fight to defend it.

Money, money, money

Meanwhile, in the other parts of the world the English were busy making money from trade. Popular items were bought from aboard, where they were cheap, and brought back to England where they could be sold for a high price.

A number of rich businessmen formed groups – or companies – to trade all over the world. With special permission from Queen Elizabeth, the **Moscow Company** brought wood, tar and rope from Russia while the **East India Company** brought rugs, spices and jewels from India. It looked as if trade and empire were here to stay!

Work

1 Each of these dates is important in the early years of Britain's Empire: 1583; 1590; 1492; 1497; 1559; 1587; 1584; 1577.
Write down the dates in order. Beside each, write what happened in that year.

2 In your own words, explain how each of the following got their names:
• The New World • Newfoundland
• The Virginia colony.

MISSION ACCOMPLISHED?

• Can you explain why the first settlers went to live in North America and why these first few settlements failed?

BRITISH AMERICA

As far as Europeans were concerned, before 1492, the known world consisted of Europe, Africa and Asia. However, all that changed when Columbus accidentally discovered the Americas (he thought he was on his way to China or India, remember!). In the years that followed, all sorts of countries claimed land in the Americas and England began to dominate North America (what we now know as the USA and Canada). This Depth Study looks at how that happened. It studies how the first successful colonists managed to survive, why the number of British settlers grew, how the local tribes reacted to this 'European invasion', and finally how the British eventually 'lost' America as it gained its independence.

1: Jamestown 1607: Are you tough enough?

MISSION OBJECTIVES

- To find out why English people first settled in America.
- To understand how difficult they found their new life to begin with.

After a few failed attempts to settle in North America a new colony called Jamestown was established in Virginia in 1607. This colony survived – but would you have been tough enough to live there? Read the following story carefully – and look through the sources – before attempting the work section at the end.

14 May 1607

James I became King of England after his cousin, Queen Elizabeth I, died in 1603. In 1606 he gave permission for a group of businessmen to set up the Virginia Company. Their aim was to sail to Virginia, establish a settlement, and see if the land was fit to grow crops. They were also on the lookout for gold! By December 1606 the settlers, sailors, ships and businessmen were ready and around 150 people set sail for America – which they reached on 14 May 1607. Forty-five people died on the voyage. The settlers quickly built a fort and other buildings, which they named 'Jamestown' after the king.

↰ SOURCE A: *Arrival at Jamestown.*

'Twenty or thirty went ashore but were assaulted by the Indians who charged at them. Captain Archer and Matthew Morton were shot with arrows but Captain Newport shot back at them with his pistol. Having shot all their arrows, the Indians fled. At that place we made our choice to build a great city, then everything was brought ashore and we quickly began to build our fort.'

↲ SOURCE B: *Written by Captain John Smith, one of the early settlers in Virginia. From 'A True Relation of Occurrences and Accidents in Virginia' by John Smith, 1608.*

Life in the New World

Life for the settlers was tough – very tough. For a start, many of them were 'gentlemen' who had never built anything or farmed in their lives. They struggled to grow crops properly and soon suffered from starvation. Diseases like malaria were a problem, and there was the issue of the natives too. Sometimes they got on well with the local tribes – but at other times they fought. In fact, by 1609, only 60 of the original settlers were still alive!

'The land can easily sustain us – there are plenty of fish, deer, stags and rabbits, with many fruits and roots good for meat. There are valleys and plains streaming with sweet springs, there are hills and mountains full of hidden treasure not yet searched.'

⤶ SOURCE E: *A picture claiming to show what life was like for settlers in America.*

Success at last

Despite all the setbacks, the settlers who survived were determined to stay. Together with new arrivals – and with help from the friendlier natives – they began to farm the land properly. One of the main crops the settlers grew was tobacco. It was easy to grow and brought in lots of money. Smoking was becoming more and more popular in Europe so the settlers sent it back 'home' to sell.

And once the money started flowing into Jamestown, the colony grew as more and more people left England to make their fortune in the New World. Soon settlements sprang up all over Virginia – the British were there to stay!

'It is inhabited by wild and savage people that live all over the forests. They have no law but native and wear clothes made from the skin of beasts and some go naked. The better sorts have houses, but poor ones have neither Arts nor Science, but are generally loving and gentle and do entertain us with kindness. They are easy to be brought to good but would happily like better conditions.'

⤶ SOURCE C: *A description of the tribes encountered by the settlers, from 'Nova Britannia' by R.I., 1609.*

↵ SOURCE D: *A description of the land provided by the Virginia Company – who organized the voyage to Jamestown. They were desperate for more people to go out there and make their settlement a success.*

✚ Hungry for MORE

Captain John Smith, one of the original settlers, was captured by tribesmen in December 1607. He claimed his life was saved by a tribal princess called Pocahontas. Find out the real story of this remarkable woman and compare it to the Disney film.

Work

1 Look at Source B. What does the choice of building erected first tell us about the feelings and experiences of these new settlers when they arrived in America?

2 Look at Source C.
   a In your own words, describe what these new settlers witnessed when they met the 'natives'.
   b Do you think these settlers felt that they were more civilized than the natives? Explain your answer.

3 Look at Sources D and E. Do you think they give a reliable view of life in the New World? Give reasons for your answer.

____ MISSION ACCOMPLISHED? ____

• Can you explain why English people first settled in America?

The first settlers in America arrived from many different European countries including Spain, France, Sweden, Finland, Holland and Britain (see Source A)... and they all had different plans for this 'New World'! The Spanish, for example, wanted gold and new land, whilst the French were more interested in trading goods like furs and tobacco than in taking over. The British took land too, hoping to grow crops that they could sell back in Europe for high profits.

2: Life in the colonies

MISSION OBJECTIVES

- To describe how Britain came to dominate the 'New World'.

Get off my land!

With more settlers in the New World came more arguments over territory, and many disputes with Native Americans as well. For example, one island, the Caribbean island of St. Martin, was first claimed in 1493 by Christopher Columbus for Spain. Not long after, all of the native people had either been killed or turned into slaves – and then the French took over, then the Dutch, and then the British invaded. In fact, the land changed hands 12 times over the next 130 years – and even today it is still divided between the French and the Dutch!

However, by the mid-1700s Britain and France had the largest presence in the Americas. The British settlers had by now divided their land into 13 areas or colonies, whilst the French had settled mainly in the north (what we now know as Canada), the middle of America and a small area in the south (see Source B). And between 1754 and 1763, these two European nations fought each other for total control of North America!

Americans today call this the French and Indian War, whilst in Britain it is known as the Seven Years War. After years of bitter and bloody fighting, in which both sides were helped by native tribes, Britain won the war and took

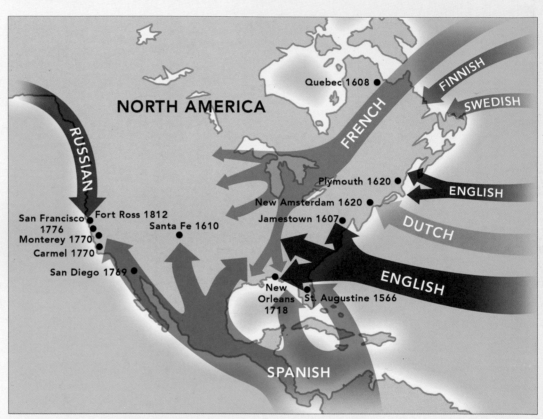

⌐ SOURCE A: *The European invasion of America.*

control of most of France's territory in the New World, including Canada. Now Britain was the dominant nation in North America.

Thirteen colonies

The part of America occupied by the British was known as the 'thirteen colonies', because there were thirteen regions or living areas along the east coast where the Brits had settled. The settlers were mostly farmers who grew crops like corn, wheat, tobacco, rice and cotton. In some areas they produced iron, paper and cloth too (see Source D).

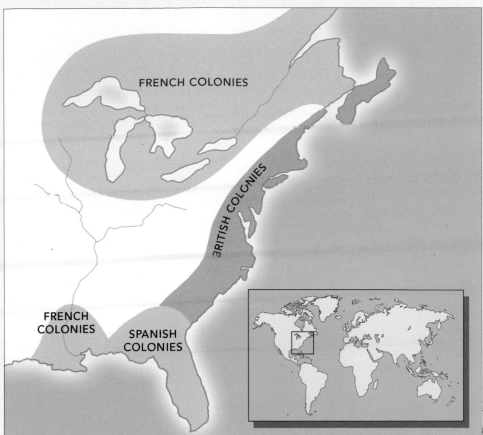

↰ SOURCE B: *How land in North America was 'roughly' divided up between the French and British (and Spanish).*

↰ SOURCE C: *The Grand Union Flag. This is seen by many as America's first flag. The 13 stripes represent the 13 colonies, whilst the Union Flag indicates their tie to England.*

Work ⟋

1 List three reasons why different European nations decided to build settlements in North America in the 1600s and 1700s.

2 **a** What was the Seven Years War?
 b What was the outcome of this conflict?

3 Look at Source C.
 a Draw Source C in your book.
 b Label your flag with its name. Underneath it, write an explanation of what the stripes represented. Why was the Union Flag included?

4 Imagine you are a settler who has briefly returned to England. Prepare a short speech to give to a group who are eager to know what life is like in the New World. Explain how Britain has come to dominate North America, tell them about the 13 colonies and describe the variety of crops grown there.

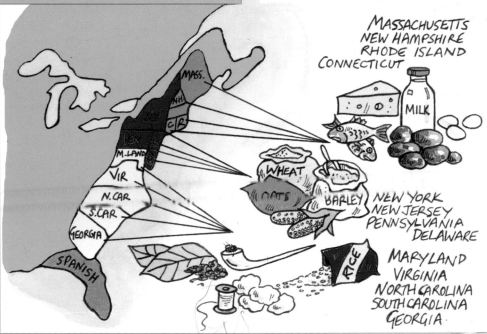

MASSACHUSETTS
NEW HAMPSHIRE
RHODE ISLAND
CONNECTICUT

NEW YORK
NEW JERSEY
PENNSYLVANIA
DELAWARE

MARYLAND
VIRGINIA
NORTH CAROLINA
SOUTH CAROLINA
GEORGIA

↰ SOURCE D: *The 13 American colonies.*

✚ ## Hungry for **MORE**

One of the most famous groups of British people to settle in America arrived in November 1620 on a ship called the 'Mayflower'. They were mainly Puritans (strict Christians) who had left Britain because they had not been free to worship God as they wished. Why not find out all you can about them? Where did they land? Did their settlement survive? And how are they remembered in America today?

── **MISSION ACCOMPLISHED?** ──

• Can you explain what is meant by the 'thirteen colonies'… and point them out on a modern world map?

• Do you know what life was like in the 13 colonies?

The idea of slavery is a very old one. The Egyptians, for example, used slaves to build the pyramids and the Romans forced them to fight in gladiator arenas. When the Spanish began to settle in the Americas in the early 1500s, they forced the native people to grow food, hunt animals, dig for gold and farm cotton. And the Spanish were very cruel to their slaves – on one Caribbean island there were around two million natives when the Spanish arrived in 1492. Sixty years later there were none left! When they ran out of slaves the Spanish had to go somewhere else to find new ones – Africa!

3: Was Britain involved in the slave trade?

MISSION OBJECTIVES

- To develop an opinion on the extent to which Britain was involved in the slave trade.

Triangular trade

The slave trade was a brutal business, which was sometimes called 'the slave triangle'. Source A and the explanation below describe how it worked.

1 Load a ship with goods that are popular in Africa – guns, cloth, iron pots and pans, copper kettles, spirits, cheap bracelets and necklaces – and sail to Africa. The goods must be cheap to buy in Europe, but highly prized in Africa.

2 Unload the ship and exchange the goods for captured slaves. The slave trader swaps a cheap cargo of goods for something that is really needed in the Americas – slaves!

3 After a gruelling two-month journey across the Atlantic Ocean, the slaves arrive to be cleaned up and sold to farmers. The slave trader will make a fortune while the slaves will go to work on the huge farms or **plantations**. The slave trader will then buy a load of sugar, cotton or tobacco and load it onto his empty ship. When he returns to Europe, he will sell his precious cargo to the cotton-wearing, sugar-loving, tobacco-smoking public… and make another huge profit!

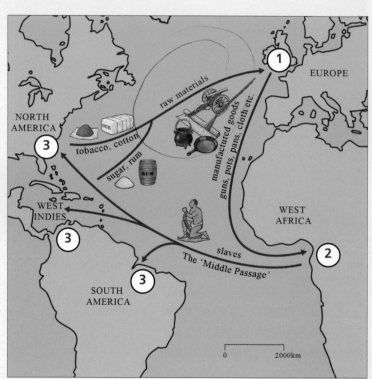

↰ SOURCE A: *How the 'slave trade' worked.*

The British get involved

From the 1560s onwards, British merchants became involved in the slave trade. One slave trader, John Hawkins, made so much money from selling slaves that he asked Queen Elizabeth herself if he could alter his family's coat of arms to include his new money-making venture! Source B shows his infamous new family crest.

↰ SOURCE B: *This was the official coat of arms for one English slave trader. He designed it himself and had these crests carved into most of his furniture in his London home!*

Slaves in America

In 1619 the first African slaves arrived in the British colony of Virginia in America. The African men, women and children had been taken from the west coast of Africa to work on the huge farms that grew tobacco, cotton and sugar. Official figures show that between 1690 and 1787, over 11,000 British ships took slaves to the Americas. Many Brits played a significant part in the slave trade – ship owners, slave traders and slave owners, for example.

SOURCE C: *African men and women being rounded up and inspected before being loaded onto a slave ship bound for America.*

There were many other British people who were also linked in some way to this trade in human beings – dock workers unloading ships full of cotton that the slaves had grown, factory workers turning the slave cotton into shirts, and even the shop owners selling sugar and tobacco. Ports like Bristol and Liverpool grew into large cities during the slave trade – and many of their fine buildings that still stand today were built with the profits from slavery. In fact, a well known actor of the time, George Frederick Cooke, once said: 'Every brick in the city of Liverpool is cemented with the blood of a slave!'

A life of slavery

Farming tobacco, cotton and sugar is incredibly hard work and the British farmers in America didn't want to do it… they'd much sooner buy a slave to do it. Between 1518 and 1800, over 11 million Africans were taken from their homes and forced to become slaves in America and the Caribbean.

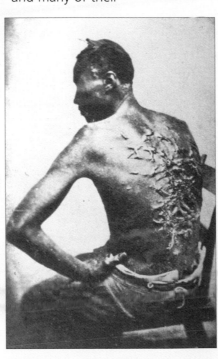

A slave would be expected to work for most of his or her life. Three- and four-year-olds would work in 'trash gangs' (weeding) or as water-can carriers. Between the ages of nine and twelve, they would start to work in the fields with the adults. As they got older, slaves would often do less exhausting jobs, such as gardening, horse-and-carriage driving, cooking, cleaning or nursing. However, hard work, a poor diet, tough punishments and no proper medical attention meant that few slaves lived to any great age. Shockingly, the average life expectancy of a slave was 26.

Slaves had no legal rights. They weren't allowed to learn to read or write, marry, or own property. As you might imagine, some slaves tried to run away but this was a very risky business as they could easily be caught. Special teams of 'runaway hunters' scoured the countryside looking for them. Any runaway slaves were severely punished (see Sources D and E).

PUNISHMENTS FOR SLAVES WHO BREAK MY LAWS

For any rebellions: rebels nailed to the ground then burnt; fire applied starting at the feet, gradually moving up to the head.

For continued running away: removal of hand, foot or testicles with an axe.

For running away: neck ring or iron **muzzle**

Failing to do duties properly: lashed for every year of the slave's life.

R Kennedy, plantation owner, Jamaica 1767

SOURCE D: *Based on a report by a visitor to a plantation.*

SOURCE E: *A photograph of an escaped slave named Gordon.*

Work

1 a Why did European settlers in the Americas want slaves?
  b In total, how many Africans were taken to become slaves in America and the Caribbean?
  c In your own words, explain how the slave trade was organized. Use a diagram to help you.

2 Look through the text to find the quote from George Frederick Cooke. What do you think he meant?

3 Look at Sources D and E.
  a Why do you think many slave owners treated their slaves so badly, especially when they tried to escape?
  b List five facts about a typical slave's life on a plantation.

MISSION ACCOMPLISHED?

• Can you answer each of these questions: how, why and when did Britain get involved in the slave trade?

DEPTH STUDY
BRITISH AMERICA

By the 1700s many British settlers in America were getting upset about all the interference from the politicians back home in Britain. For example, the settlers had to sell all their important goods, such as cotton, tobacco and copper, directly to Britain and nowhere else. And if they wanted to buy anything from other countries, the goods had to go to Britain first… where they were taxed! The colonists had to pay tax on paint, glass, coffee, wine, sugar… even newspapers! Some colonists felt no connection to Britain either – they had been born in America and regarded themselves as Americans! In fact, some settlers wanted to break free from British rule and run America themselves – they wanted independence!

4: Revolution

MISSION OBJECTIVES

• To understand why America finally declared independence from Britain.
• To understand what is meant by the Boston Tea Party and the Declaration of Independence.

I want to break free

As resentment grew in America about the taxes payable to the British government, a conflict began to build. They were especially upset when the Brits taxed their cups of tea – three pence to Britain for every pound of tea sold in America. As a protest, a group of unhappy Americans (dressed as Native Americans) boarded three British ships in Boston and dumped 342 crates full of tea (£11,000-worth) into the harbour (see Sources A and B).

↖ **SOURCE A:** *The 'Boston Tea Party'. Americans today are very proud of the actions of their ancestors in 1773. They see it as a great example of how far Americans are prepared to go to speak out for their freedom.*

There was an old lady lived over the sea

There was an old lady lived over the sea
And she was an Island Queen.
Her daughter lived off in a new countrie,
With an ocean of water between.
The old lady's pockets were full of gold
But never contented was she,
So she called on her daughter to pay her a tax
Of three pence a pound on her tea.
'Now mother, dear mother,' the daughter replied,
'I shan't do the thing you ax.
I'm willing to pay a fair price for the tea,
But never the three penny tax.'
'You shall,' quoth the mother, and reddened with rage,
'For you're my own daughter, you see,
And sure, 'tis quite proper the daughter should pay
Her mother a tax on her tea.'
And so the old lady her servant called up
And packed off a budget of tea,
And eager for three pence a pound, she put
In enough for a large family.
She order'd her servants to bring home the tax,
Declaring her child should obey,
Or old as she was, and almost woman grown,
She'd half whip her life away.
The tea was conveyed to the daughter's door,
All down by the ocean's side,
And the bouncing girl pour'd out every pound
In the dark and boiling tide.
And then she called out to the Island Queen,
'O mother, dear mother,' quoth she,
'Your tea you may have when 'tis steep'd enough
But never a tax from me.'

↖ **SOURCE B:** *An American song written after the Boston Tea Party.*

The British responded to the 'Boston Tea Party' by closing the whole port of Boston… which angered the Americans even more. So when the British banned all town meetings, the Americans began meeting in secret. In September 1774, 56 representatives from the colonies met in Philadelphia to decide what to do. This meeting is known as the 'First Congress' (and even today, American Parliament is still known as 'Congress'). Delegates at the First Congress decided to fight the Brits!

It's war!

The British sent soldiers to force the American rebels to stay loyal to Britain. They were met with fierce resistance. In July 1775 the Americans appointed George Washington as the leader of their army – he would go on to become their first President and have the capital city named after him.

A year later, in July 1776, Congress met again and formally declared themselves independent from Britain (see Source C).

America wins

After over five years of bitter fighting, in which thousands of soldiers from both sides died, the Americans finally won. When he found out about the defeat, the British Prime Minister at the time (Lord North) broke down and cried. The 13 colonies then joined together to form the United States of America. They even got themselves a new flag (see Source E)! In 1789 this new independent country appointed its first President, George Washington. And so this valuable colony was lost by Britain forever!

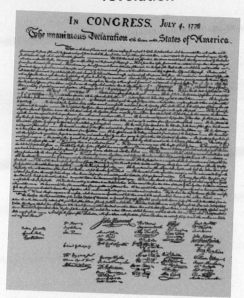

↰ SOURCE C: *The Declaration of Independence, signed 4 July 1776, which is now known as Independence Day.*

↰ SOURCE D: *The leader of the British Army, Lord Cornwallis, surrendering to the leader of the American Army, General George Washington, in October 1781.*

↰ SOURCE E: *The first ever flag of the USA was made up of 13 stars and 13 stripes – to symbolize the 13 colonies.*

Work

1 Imagine you are an angry American in 1773. Write to your cousin in Britain explaining why Americans are unhappy with the British government, and what the Boston Tea Party was all about!

2 Look at Source B
   a Who or what is the 'old lady' who 'lived over the sea'? Who is the 'daughter'?
   b Write out the two lines that refer to the Boston Tea Party.

3 Write down what happened in America in each of the following five years: 1773; 1774; 1775; 1776; 1781.

4 Americans today call the Declaration of Independence one of their 'founding documents'. What do you think this means?

—— MISSION ACCOMPLISHED? ——

• Can you explain why the first US flag had 13 stars and 13 stripes?

! FACT What about Canada?

America broke away from British rule in 1776 – but the colonies to the north, in what we now call Canada, stayed part of the British Empire. These huge colonies, such as Quebec, Ontario, New Brunswick and Nova Scotia, remained a key part of the Empire for nearly a century – until they achieved 'self-government' (the right to run most of their own affairs) in 1867.

Should Britain make up for its role in slavery?

─── MISSION OBJECTIVES ───

• To form your own opinion – should Britain pay compensation for its role in the slave trade... or not?

In September 2001 a world conference was held in South Africa to discuss the topic of racism. One of the topics discussed was the slave trade – in particular, whether nations who had used slaves in their colonies many years ago should apologize for doing so. Some representatives there asked for these nations to recognize that their involvement in the slave trade was a 'crime against humanity' – and suggested that they should think about paying compensation to the African countries from which the slaves were taken!

The topic of 'slavery compensation' sparked discussion and debate all over the world, making headlines in newspapers and on TV news programmes. So what do *you* think? What are the arguments for and against the idea of compensation for the slave trade? How did the slave trade itself actually end? And how did Britain's politicians respond to the issues raised at the conference?

Slavery and the Empire

Britain first got involved in the slave trade in the 1500s. It was certainly not the only European nation involved in the trade but Britain made some of the largest profits from it! By the 1700s the transportation of African slaves to parts of the Empire such as America and the West Indies had turned into a huge money-making business. Even Queen Elizabeth herself was a business partner of John Hawkins, one of the best known Tudor slave dealers (and often called 'the father of the slave trade'). King Charles II was a partner in the Royal African Company, a business that transported 70,000 slaves from Africa between 1680 and 1688... 48,000 of whom died on the journey to the West Indies.

A profitable trade

An estimated three million African slaves were bought and sold between 1630 and 1807, generating profits of about £12 million (which would be equivalent to more than £1 billion today). This money helped Britain become one of the richest and most powerful nations in the world. Certainly, many of the fine buildings in Liverpool and Bristol (and also London to some extent) were built on the profits of slavery. Even Penny Lane – the Liverpool street made famous by the 1967 Beatles' hit – is reputed to have been named after a slave ship owner named James Penny!

↰ **SOURCE A:** *A 1634 painting of Princess Henrietta, the youngest daughter of King Charles I of England. Black servants, brought to England as slaves, often appeared in paintings at this time. In some paintings they are grouped with the family's pets or horses, a sign of their status in the house!*

↵ **SOURCE B:** *A close-up of one of the sculptures that decorate Liverpool Town Hall. The building is covered in sculptures showing Liverpool's African trading links, and was built with money from people who had made their fortunes through the slave trade. As many as 16 of Liverpool's mayors between 1787 and 1807 are thought to have been slave merchants.*

In fact, many Brits played a significant part in the slave trade – ship owners (who allowed their ships to be used), bankers (who lent them the money), investors (who shared in the profits) and importers (who brought in the tobacco, sugar and cotton that the slaves farmed). Yet Britain's link to slavery goes even further. For example, the world-famous National Gallery in London received its first major donation of paintings from a man who had built up his art collection with the money he made from slave dealing. And several of the men who ran the Bank of England in the early years were involved in slavery too. Clearly, then, Britain's link to slavery runs deep, and there was a terrible human cost involved in the wealth that the slave trade brought… which is why, in recent years, there have been demands for compensation for Britain's role in it all!

'If our slave trade had gone,
There's an end to our lives,
Beggars all we be,
Our children, our wives.'

↵ **SOURCE C:** A well-known rhyme of the 1700s.

↳ **SOURCE D:** *Olaudah Equiano, a former slave who managed to buy his freedom. He moved to Britain where he married and wrote his life story. His book was a bestseller and turned many people against slavery. The fact that he was clearly intelligent and articulate made a nonsense out of claims that Africans were inferior and only good for manual work.*

The end of the slave trade in the British Empire

In the second half of the eighteenth century, pressure grew and grew to end the slave trade. In 1797 a group of 12 devout Christian men, led by William Wilberforce, formed a group to fight for the **abolition** of slavery. Wilberforce was a politician and made many speeches against slavery in Parliament. Another member of the group, Thomas Clarkson, collected together evidence of the horrors of the slave trade and the treatment the slaves faced. He talked to sailors, inspected ships… and even collected objects that were used to punish slaves. Anti-slavery campaigners also published pictures like the one shown in Source E to show how terribly slaves were treated.

SOURCE E: *This horrific image shows how many slaves could be packed into the slave ship* Brookes. *This picture first appeared on an anti-slavery poster designed to demonstrate the terrors of the slave trade.* ↰

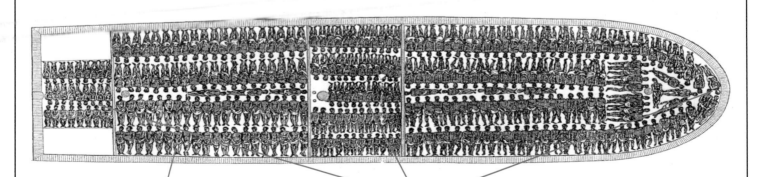

- Slaves shackled together in rows, lying on their backs or sides. Most had only approximately 30cm of space around them.

- The diagram shows how some of the 482 slaves were packed into the ship. On one occasion the Brookes carried 609 slaves.

- Men were loaded in the bow (front of the ship), boys in the centre and women and young girls in the stern (back).

- Food and water were kept in the hold below the slaves. It was rationed so it would last the whole journey.

The compensation debate

For many years there have been discussions, debates – even arguments – about the issue of compensation for the slave trade. Some argue that the countries that were involved in the trade – and made money from it – should pay compensation to the African nations from which the men, women and children were taken.

Others argue that compensation should not be paid because no one is left alive who profited from slavery – or who suffered directly as a result of it. Below are some different opinions about the 'compensation debate' – which ones do you agree with?

'Slavery was racist – it depended on the belief that white people were better than other races. That belief is wrong – plain and simple! People should never have been allowed to own others... what about human rights? Aren't we all created equal?'

'The countries that made money out of slavery should help the ancestors of those slaves in Africa today. It doesn't have to be money – but perhaps they could provide education, medical care, irrigation schemes and so on.'

'The compensation would have to come out of taxes, paid for by the British public. Is it really fair for people in modern Britain to pay for something that happened so long ago? People today shouldn't be made to feel guilty about something that a different generation did!'

'Where would it end? Should Denmark pay compensation to Britain for attacks by the Vikings? Or the Queen to Catholics for the closing of the Catholic monasteries by Henry VIII? No one is left alive today who made money out of slavery – or who personally suffered from it!'

'The slave trade destroyed Africa. The traders took the young, strong Africans – and left the old, weak and sick. Africa never recovered! Slavery helped make Britain rich – at the expense of Africa. Britain owes Africa for this!'

A B C D E

Britain's response

When the topic of the slave trade came up at the World Conference on Racism, Britain's politicians there were asked repeatedly for their thoughts and opinions. In the end, the British Government refused to apologize for Britain's role in the slave trade, instead saying only that they 'expressed regret about the slave trade'! They were not prepared to call slavery 'a crime against humanity' and did not want to pay any money in compensation to African nations. However, the majority of countries at the Conference *did* call the slave trade a 'crime against humanity' – though they didn't ask Britain to pay any money.

Interestingly, on the 200th anniversary of the abolition of the slave trade in the British Empire in 2007, Prime Minister Tony Blair said that the slave trade was 'shameful' and that 'Britain expresses its deep sorrow that it could ever have happened and rejoices at the better times we live in today'. Perhaps the debate about whether Britain should pay compensation for its role in the suffering of slaves will go on and on!

'The slaves were treated so badly – families were ripped apart and African villages were devastated. Surely someone must pay for that!'

'Loads of other countries were involved in the slave trade too – but Britain stopped slavery first, and then spent the next 100 years trying to get other countries to stop!'

'Many of the slaves were criminals in their own tribes – sold into slavery by their tribal leaders. So it wasn't just whites who were involved in the slave trade.'

F

G

H

WISE-UP Words

abolition

Work

1 Make a list of ways in which Britain was linked to the slave trade. The links could be through the Royal Family, British cities, slave traders or bankers.

2 Look at Source C. In your opinion, is the writer of this rhyme for or against the slave trade? Give reasons.

3 a What is meant by the word 'abolition'?

   b Write a sentence or two about the role played in the abolition of slavery by the following people:
   • William Wilberforce
   • Thomas Clarkson
   • Olaudah Equiano.

4 a Look at the arguments for and against paying compensation labelled A–H. Sort them into two groups – those that support the idea and those that don't.

   b Now it's time to form your own opinion. Should Britain pay compensation for its role in the slave trade? Write an extended answer to this and include:
   • an introduction to the 'compensation debate'
   • the arguments for and against paying compensation
   • your own opinion – whether you favour paying compensation or not, and why.

—**MISSION ACCOMPLISHED?**—

• Can you outline at least three reasons why you think Britain *should* pay compensation for its role in the slave trade, and at least three reasons why it *shouldn't*?

INDIA

At one point there were over 50 colonies in the British Empire. They were dotted all over the world and made the British Empire the largest the world had ever known. One of the largest of these 'possessions' was India. It was the colony that many Britons treasured most, calling it the 'Jewel in the Crown' of Britain's Empire. This Depth Study looks at the reasons why the British were so proud of India, how it became part of the Empire in the first place – and how, after hundreds of years of British influence and rule, India won its independence in 1947.

1: India before the Brits

MISSION OBJECTIVES

• To be able to explain what India was like before the British took over.

Incredible India

India today is an independent country. It's the seventh largest country in the world – and the second most populated. Modern India borders Pakistan, China, Bangladesh and Nepal. India itself is a subcontinent, which means it is a huge mass of land attached to the main continent of Asia.

SOURCE A: *India today compared with India around 1500, before Europeans began setting up trading stations there. Note that the modern-day countries that surround India (Pakistan and Bangladesh, for example) are not there on the early map. Back then, the whole of the subcontinent was known as 'India'.*

India in 1500

The Indian Subcontinent today

SOURCE B: Brihadeeswarar Hindu Temple in Thanjavur. Hinduism originated in India.

SOURCE C: Mahabodhi Buddhist Temple in Bodh Gaya. Buddhism originated in India too.

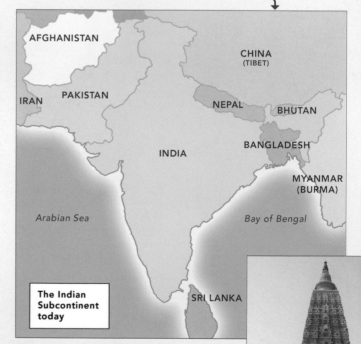

Conquest

People from all over the world have visited India, or tried to conquer it. The Persians and Iranians settled in India in ancient times. Genghis Khan invaded and looted it – and so did Alexander the Great. The Chinese came to India in pursuit of knowledge and to visit the ancient Indian universities. Then came the French... and finally the Brits!

SOURCE D: *The Golden Temple in Amritsar – the holiest place of worship for Sikhs.*

↵ **SOURCE E:** *Akbar the Great.*

Raw materials

India is rich in natural resources – iron ore, copper, gold, silver, gemstones, tea and timber. Spices (which were very valuable in the Middle Ages) were common in India too. This meant that any country that made strong trade links with India could potentially become very rich and powerful... but even more rich and powerful if they managed to take over the whole country!

A divided nation?

Three of the world's major religions – Hinduism, Buddhism and Sikhism – originated in India. Other religions, such as Judaism, Christianity and Islam, have since arrived there too. At various times throughout India's history, science, technology, engineering, art, literature, mathematics, astronomy and religion have flourished there.

By the early 1500s (when many European nations began to sail to India to trade) the subcontinent was divided into lots of kingdoms (see Source A). Most were run by Hindu princes. Occasionally the kingdoms would go to war against each other – but there were long peaceful periods too. Ruling over all the Hindu princes was the Mughal Emperor. The Mughals, who were Muslims, had invaded India in the early 1500s. Within decades the great Mughal Emperor, Akbar, had managed to unite many of the Indian states. He was well known for his knowledge of literature, great architecture and religious tolerance.

His grandson, Shah Jahan, who also became Emperor, built the famous Taj Mahal, one of the most beautiful buildings in the world. He built it in memory of his third wife – who died giving birth to their fourteenth child! However, Shah Jahan's son, Aurang Zeb, was a fanatical Muslim and picked on followers of India's other religions. As wars broke out all over India, the Mughals eventually lost control of the country. It was at exactly this time (when much of India was at war) that European nations became *very* interested in it!

↑ **SOURCE F:** *The Taj Mahal.*

Here come the Europeans

Several European nations saw these wars in India as an opportunity to increase their own power. Many nations, but mainly the Dutch, French and British, realized that by helping certain Indian princes (with weapons and soldiers, for example), they could turn the wars any way they wanted. Then when their new ally beat the enemy, they could demand rewards from the prince – perhaps land or goods! Further, if they ever fell out with him and fought against him, they usually ended up winning... and taking his territory!

Work

1 Plan a PowerPoint® presentation called 'What was India like before the British takeover?' Include details of India's eventful history and rich culture, and explain why European nations took an interest in it. Include text and pictures. Use no more than 100 words and five slides.

___ MISSION ACCOMPLISHED? ___

- In no more than 100 words, can you explain what India was like before the British arrived?

In 1497 a Portuguese explorer called Vasco da Gama discovered how to get to India by sea. Soon many European countries were sending ships to India to trade. At first the ships simply reached an Indian port, bartered or swapped their goods with local traders for silk, spices, cotton or tea, and brought these back to their own country to sell for a big profit. After a few years, and with the permission of local Indian rulers, the traders began to set up permanent trading stations. These were large warehouses surrounded by huge fences and guarded by men with guns. All the goods were stored in the warehouse and this was where all the trading took place. Sometimes the traders lived there with their families too.

2: An Indian takeaway

MISSION OBJECTIVES

- To find out how 'trading' worked… and how one of the world's best-known trading companies came to dominate India by the 1850s.

The East India Company

The British, French and Dutch were the main countries with trading stations in India in the early years, but the Danish and Portuguese traded there too (see Sources A and B).

! FACT India itself
Today, India is a single, independent country. However, when the British first started trading there, people used the word 'India' to mean the present-day countries of Pakistan, Burma (also known as Myanmar), Bangladesh and Sri Lanka too. The British gave the name India to the whole lot!

The British trading stations in India were all run by one company – the East India Company. Set up in 1600, it had been sending ships all over the world for years. The ships sailed full of cheap British goods, and swapped them for goods in countries as far away as Japan and China. Then they brought the fine china, silk, coffee and spices back to Britain to sell for a huge profit. Both the businessmen in charge of the company, and the kings and queens to whom they paid taxes, made a fortune from this trade (see Source C).

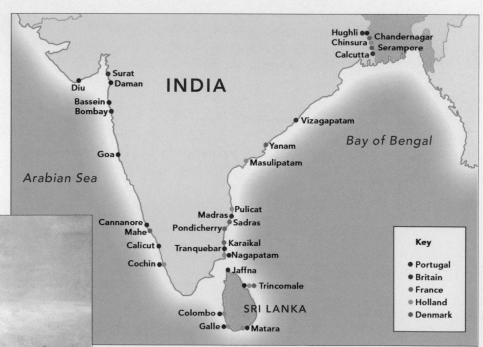

Key
- Portugal
- Britain
- France
- Holland
- Denmark

⤴ SOURCE A: *India's trading ports – and the European nations who founded them.*

⤵ SOURCE B: *This is the British trading station at Bombay in 1731.*

Stage 1: Get a group of rich businessmen together... and buy a ship.

WELL THERE SHE IS!

THE FIRST OF MANY VOYAGES I HOPE

I HOPE SHE DOESN'T SINK

Stage 2: Load the ship with goods wanted in India – guns, ammunition, swords, tools, buttons and shoes.

MOST OF THESE GOODS ARE OLD AND SECOND HAND!

THEY ARE DESPERATE FOR THIS STUFF OVER THERE

Stage 3: Sail to India.

I FEEL SEASICK

Stage 4: Unload the goods at the trading station – and swap them for things that are cheap and easy to get in India but hard to get in Britain!

SILK SPICES TEA COTTON

Stage 5: Sail back to Britain with your fully loaded ship.

I'M STILL SEASICK

Stage 6: Sell the Indian goods in Britain – for far more than you paid for the British goods you swapped them for!

WHAT A GREAT WAY TO MAKE MONEY

THE EAST INDIA COMPANY IS THE ONLY BRITISH COMPANY ALLOWED TO TRADE IN INDIA

LET'S DO IT AGAIN!

⤴ **SOURCE C:** *How to make a fortune from trade.*

The East India Company first set up trading posts in India in Surat (1612), Madras (1638) and Bombay (1668). In the 1700s the East India Company began to take more and more Indian land. It had its own private army and navy and used them against the various regional rulers of India. At the Battle of Plassey in 1757, for example, around 3000 Company troops (2200 of whom were local Indians) defeated an Indian army of over 40,000 led by local prince Siraj-ud-Daulah (who was even helped by the French!). This allowed the East India Company to take over Bengal, the area formerly ruled by Siraj, and one of the richest parts of India. The Company fought against other European nations too – and took over their trading posts!

The Company expands

Over the following decades, the various Indian princes and rulers were either beaten in battle or played off against each other, so that more and more of India came under British rule. In fact, by the mid-1850s most of India was controlled by the Brits… but a major rebellion, one that shocked the world, was just around the corner!

Work

1 a What is a 'trading station'?
  b List the European countries that set up trading stations in India in the 1600s.
  c What was the East India Company?
  d Explain how this Company gradually took control of most of India.
2 Create your own diagram, poster or leaflet explaining how Brits made money from trading with India. Use Source C to inspire you!

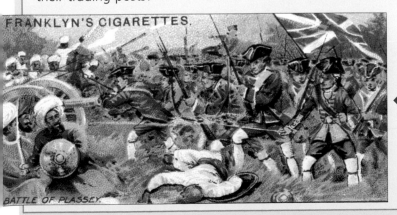

FRANKLYN'S CIGARETTES.

BATTLE OF PLASSEY.

⤶ **SOURCE D:** *A picture of the East India Company's victory at Plassey. They were led by Robert Clive, a Company worker.*

__ MISSION ACCOMPLISHED? __
• Can you recall five facts about the East India Company?

By the 1850s, most of India was ruled by the British. The East India Company had gradually taken more and more land and many of the British people who worked for the Company lived in great luxury in India and made huge fortunes. To help 'protect' them whilst out in India – and to make sure things ran smoothly – British soldiers were stationed all over India. The army recruited local Indians as soldiers to help them. However, on 10 May 1857, Indian soldiers (called '**Sepoys**') working for the Brits in Meerut (northern India) shot dead a number of British soldiers who worked with them. Soon the whole of northern India was engulfed in a ferocious fight between Brits and Sepoys. This is known as the Indian **Mutiny**… or the War of Independence! So what caused the uprising? How did the Brits respond? And why does the same event have different names?

3: Indian Mutiny... or a War of Independence?

—————————————— **MISSION OBJECTIVES** ——————————————

• To understand how the events of 1857–1858 can be interpreted differently.

Suffering Sepoys

According to Queen Victoria herself, the aim of the British Empire was to 'protect the poor natives and advance civilization'. In India, the Brits claimed that they were *improving* India (rather than exploiting it) by building railways, roads, schools and hospitals.

However, in the army, the Sepoys were a very unhappy bunch. They felt that they weren't treated very well, had little hope of promotion and were often the first to be sent to the most dangerous places. Some Sepoys also felt that they were being pressured into converting to Christianity.

This build-up of anger boiled over into rebellion in 1857, when a new rifle was delivered to the troops with a new method of loading the bullets. And it was these new bullets, and the **cartridges** that held them, that led to the start of the Empire's most bloody rebellion!

! FACT Hindus and Muslims
In the 1850s, the British Army in India was made up of 200,000 Sepoys (mainly Hindus and Muslims) and 40,000 British.

! FACT Not the first!
The Sepoy rebellion of 1857 was not the first rebellion in India. In 1806, in the town of Vellore in southern India, a rebellion broke out when the Brits banned Hindu Sepoys from wearing religious marks on their foreheads and made Muslim Sepoys shave their beards and trim their moustaches. After a day of violence (in which 200 British troops were killed or injured) the revolt was crushed, with over 800 rebels dying in the process.

SOURCE A: *Indian Sepoys in the British Army.* ➤

The spark

In January 1857, a new Enfield rifle was given to each Indian soldier. The bullet (which fired from the rifle) and the gunpowder that fired it were neatly packaged together in a cartridge (see Source B).

Loading the cartridge was a rather complicated affair. It involved biting off the top of the cartridge, pouring the gunpowder into the gun and then ramming the rest of the cartridge (with the bullet inside) down into the gun. The problem for the Hindu and Muslim Sepoys was that the new cartridges were covered in grease to make them slide down the gun barrel easily. And because the soldier had to bite off the top of the greasy cartridge in order to get to the gunpowder, it meant that the Sepoys got grease in their mouths. It was rumoured that the grease was made from animal fat, probably (but not definitely) a mixture of pork and beef fat – the worst possible mixture for Hindus and Muslims. After all, Hindus can't eat beef because to them a cow is sacred… and Muslims are forbidden to eat pork!

The Sepoys objected to the new cartridges – but were largely ignored. And when 85 Sepoys refused to use the cartridges they were arrested and sent to jail for ten years. Days later, other Sepoys rioted in support of their imprisoned comrades – and soon the whole of northern India was engulfed in rebellion.

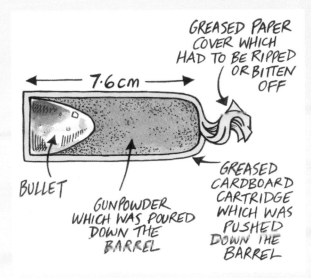

GREASED PAPER COVER WHICH HAD TO BE RIPPED OR BITTEN OFF

7.6 cm

BULLET

GUNPOWDER WHICH WAS POURED DOWN THE BARREL

GREASED CARDBOARD CARTRIDGE WHICH WAS PUSHED DOWN THE BARREL

⌐ **SOURCE B:** *An Enfield rifle cartridge.*

Work

1 What is a Sepoy?

2 a Copy the diagram in Source B. Underneath write a short explanation of what a cartridge is.

b Carefully explain what caused the 1857 rebellion. You need to include what the British did in January 1857 – and why Hindu and Muslim Sepoys objected so strongly.

⌐ **SOURCE C:** *The Siege of Lucknow. British soldiers in Lucknow (northern India) were surrounded and attacked by Indian rebels on 1 July 1857. The siege finally ended when support for the British arrived in November.*

India at war

The main battles were fought in Delhi, Cawnpore and Lucknow (see Source C). The massacre of 200 British women and children at Cawnpore outraged the British. Back home in Britain crowds bayed for blood (see Source D). Even Queen Victoria was horrified. Soon, 70,000 fresh troops were sent to India armed with the latest Colt revolvers made in America. And revenge was violent, bloody and swift!

When some Muslim mutineers were captured they were sewn into pig skins before they were hanged, whilst others were forced to clean up blood by licking it off the floor. One British soldier wrote of a giant tree with 130 Sepoys hanging from its branches. Especially horrible was the British punishment of being blown from the barrel of a gun – captured rebels were strapped to cannons, which were then fired! (see Source E).

'And England, now avenge their wrongs by vengeance deep and dire,
Cut out their cancer with the sword, and burn it out with fire,
Destroy those traitor regions, hang every pariah hound,
And hunt them down to death, in all hills and cities around.'

↵ **SOURCE D:** *A British poem by Martin Tupper, written at the time of the Mutiny.*

↰ **SOURCE E:** *A painting showing the brutal punishment of rebel Sepoys.*

↵ **SOURCE F:** *Lakshmibai, the Rani (Queen) of Jhansi, an area of northern India. Born in 1828, she lost much of her land to the British and fought against them in 1857. She died during the Battle of Gwalior in June 1858 (although her body was never found). Even the British said of her that she was 'remarkable for her beauty, cleverness and determination' and had been 'the most dangerous of the rebel leaders'. She is referred to often today as India's Joan of Arc and there are two bronze statues of her in Jhansi and Gwalior. The Indian National Army even named its first female unit after her!*

! FACT **All Sepoys?**
The majority of Sepoys took part in the rebellion – but not all of them. Thousands, including the Gurkhas, the Sikhs and the Pathan regiments, remained loyal to the Brits. Even today the Gurkhas who fight in the British Army have an astonishing reputation for loyalty to it!

The end... and after

Peace was finally declared on 8 July 1858, but the 'mutiny' had shocked the British. For a long time it had looked as if the British might be defeated – and politicians were taken aback by the ferocity of feeling that had been shown against the British in India.

After the mutiny, the British were a lot more careful about how they governed India. They still wanted India as part of the Empire (of course), but the running of the country was taken away from the East India Company and replaced with direct rule by the British Government. A new government department (the India Office) was set up and a **viceroy** was put in charge of India on behalf of Queen Victoria herself.

Before the mutiny, the British policy in India was to introduce British ideas about religion and education – which threatened the Hindu, Muslim and Sikh ways of life. After 1858, the British tried to interfere less with religious matters, and started to allow Indians more say in the running of India by allowing them jobs in local government. Even Queen Victoria commented on the new way of running India (see Source G). However, by 1900, nine out of ten jobs running the country were still done by Brits.

What's in a name?

Historians like to give names to different periods of time (the Ice Age, the Middle Ages, the Tudor period and so on) and to different events (the Peasants' Revolt, the English Civil War) – but no one seems to be able to agree over what to call the events of 1857–1858. At the time in Britain it was known as the 'Indian Mutiny' or the 'Sepoy Rebellion'. It is often still called this in Britain today. However, for Indians and Pakistanis today, it is referred to as 'The War of Independence' or the 'Great Rebellion'. It is looked upon as the first episode in the great struggle against the British for a free India. Indeed, in 2007 the Indian and Pakistani governments celebrated the 150th anniversary of the Rebellion of 1857 with special events and ceremonies. On the official Indian government website, it is called 'The Great Rebellion' and is contained in a section entitled 'The Indian Freedom Struggle' (see Source H).

'The Hindus, Muslims and Sikhs and all the other brave sons of India fought shoulder to shoulder to throw out the British.'

⤷ **SOURCE H:** *A quote from the official Indian government website, india.gov.in.*

'1857 was a pivotal point in Indian history... the better educated Indians who emerged from English-speaking schools in India, and who had learned about political parties, strikes and protest marches when they were in these schools, used these new methods against the British to gain their freedom. Had 1857 not happened, modern Indian history might have taken a quite different course.'

⤷ **SOURCE I:** *Based on a BBC interview with author William Dalrymple, September 2006.*

WISE-UP Words

cartridge   mutiny
Sepoy   viceroy

'We hold ourselves bound by the same obligations of duty which bind us to our other subjects... so it is our will that our subjects of whatever race or creed, be freely and impartially admitted to offices in our service, the duties of which they may be qualified by their education, ability and integrity, duly to discharge.'

⤷ **SOURCE G:** *Queen Victoria's Proclamation to India, November 1858.*

Work

1 a In what ways did the British punish the Indian mutineers?
  b Why do you think the punishments were so brutal?

2 a Who was Lakshmibai?
  b Why do you think she is regarded as a hero in India today?

3 How did the British change the way India was governed as a result of the events of 1857?

4 Look at Source G.
  a What is Queen Victoria saying should happen in India?
  b By 1900, had her wishes been carried out?

5 a Why do you think British politicians at the time called the events of 1857 the 'Indian Mutiny'?
  b Why do you think Indians today call the same event 'The First War of Independence'?

___ MISSION ACCOMPLISHED? ___

• Can you write from two different points of view?
• What would a British Government official say about the Indian Mutiny… and what would an Indian Sepoy say?

DEPTH STUDY INDIA

India was the largest and richest of all the countries in Britain's Empire. In the 1850s a **viceroy**, appointed by the British in London, was put directly in charge of the country and ran it on behalf of Queen Victoria. The Queen even gave herself an extra title and started to call herself 'Empress of India' as well as 'Queen of Great Britain and Ireland'!

4: 'The Jewel in the Crown'

MISSION OBJECTIVES

• To identify ways that the British takeover of India could be viewed as a good thing… or a bad thing.

India was the colony that many people in Britain treasured most – even calling it 'the Jewel in the Crown'. So how did the British rule India? What was it like for Britons living there? And what was British rule like for Indians? Study the following sources carefully; they give a fascinating (and revealing) insight into British rule in India.

↑ **SOURCE A:** *Many 'Brits abroad' in India enjoyed a lifestyle far more luxurious than the one they had at home.*

'The British who lived in the colonies liked their creature comforts and were able to enjoy them more luxuriously than they generally could at home. With their hordes of servants they could live in a class above themselves.'

↑ **SOURCE B:** *From a modern history book (James Morris, 'Pax Britannica', 1968).*

↵ **SOURCE C:** *The British India flag. The term 'British Raj' was used to describe the period of British rule in India between 1858 and 1947. The word 'raj' is Hindi for 'rule'.*

↑ **SOURCE E:** *The British built thousands of miles of railway all over India. This railway station was built in Bombay (now Mumbai) in 1897. It was known as Victoria Station until 1996, when it was renamed after a seventeenth-century Hindu king.*

'Ceylon (now Sri Lanka) was unified under British rule in 1815. Over the next 80 years, the British built 2300 miles of road and 2900 miles of railway in India. The land used for farming increased from 400,000 acres to 3.2 million acres, the schools from 170 to 2900, the hospitals from 0 to 65…'

↵ **SOURCE D:** *Written by James Morris in 'Pax Britannica', 1968.*

SOURCE F: *George Nathaniel Curzon (fourth from right) was Viceroy of India from 1898 to 1905, ruling directly for Queen Victoria. This famous photograph was taken at a well-known Indian palace. Curzon is known today for doing lots of good work in India – like building schools, setting up a national irrigation system to help relieve famine and rebuilding many old Indian buildings. It was Curzon who restored the Taj Mahal to its former glory.*

WISE-UP Words

viceroy

'After every other Viceroy has been forgotten, Curzon will be remembered because he restored all that was beautiful in India.'

↳ **SOURCE G:** *A quote from the Indian leader Nehru.*

SOURCE H: *A picture of the Indian famine of the late 1800s. Approximately 6 million Indians died – and many Indians blamed the British for not doing enough. Even Florence Nightingale, the famous British nurse, said 'We do not care enough to stop them dying slow and terrible deaths from things we could easily stop. We have taken their land, and we rule it, for our good, not theirs'.* ↱

'India has become impoverished [poor] by their [Britain's] government. They take away our money from year to year. The most important jobs are reserved for themselves. We are kept in a state of slavery. They behave insolently [insultingly] towards us and disregard our feelings…'

↳ **SOURCE I:** *Written by Mohandas K. Gandhi in 'Indian Home Rule', 1938.*

Changing a nation

The issue of British control and influence in India has always been controversial and has often been interpreted differently. Some argue that India benefited from British influence in some ways. By 1900 the British had built nearly 50,000 miles of road, as well as railways, schools and hospitals. They built dams and dug nearly 70,000 miles of canal. They also introduced a new legal system and helped settle ancient feuds between rival areas and regions… whether the Indians wanted these things or not!

But India suffered too. British customs were forced on the people and local traditions, culture and religions tended to be ignored. Indian workers were often exploited, the country's raw materials were taken back to Britain, and native lands were seized… and if there was ever any resistance, the British Army usually came down very hard on the rebels.

Work

1 Write a sentence or two explaining the following terms:
- viceroy
- Empress of India
- British Raj.

2 a Make two lists, one of all the good things that British rule brought to India and one of all the negative things about British rule.

b Create a poster called 'The British in India'. Using no more than ten words (what a challenge!) show both the positives and the negatives of British rule.

MISSION ACCOMPLISHED?

- Can you write a balanced argument to answer the question: was the British takeover of India a good thing or not?

During the reign of Queen Victoria (1837–1901), the British Government had taken direct control of India, running all sorts of everyday things such as education, the army, the railways, law and order and taxation. Queen Victoria proudly called herself 'The Empress of India' and although she never actually visited India, she employed an Indian secretary to teach her Hindi and Urdu, wrote parts of her personal diary in Urdu and Hindi, employed Indian servants… and even had an Indian dish on most of her dinner menus! However, less than 50 years after Queen Victoria's death, Britain no longer controlled India – and it had been split up into independent nations that ruled themselves. So how did this happen?

5: Independence for India

MISSION OBJECTIVES

• To identify different factors that led to the 'Partition of India' in 1947.

A changing nation

There is little doubt that Britain changed India. Whether the changes were for the better or not is a matter of opinion. Some argue that the Brits 'civilized' India by building railways, roads and sewers. They built schools and universities and introduced a successful system of law and order. However, others argue that India was already a civilized nation before the Brits arrived!

Critics of British rule feel that the British left India in a worse state than when they first took over. They claim that the Brits mainly did things that would benefit Britain – and took as much of India's raw materials (cotton, tea, spices, precious jewels and so on) as they could. They say that British customs were forced on Indians, and local traditions, culture and religions were often ignored! Sources B and C illustrate the split in opinion about the Brits in India.

SOURCE A: *Queen Victoria at her desk, helped by her personal servant, Abdul Karim. The Queen was really fond of Karim, giving him land in India when she died.* ↱

'British brains, British trade, and British money changed India. Many bridges, 40,000 miles of railway, and 70,000 miles of roads show how hard the British worked. They brought water to vast areas of farmland. They built sewers, gave good wages, built canals and handed out food. As a result, famines almost ended.'

↰ **SOURCE B:** *Adapted from 'The English in India' by British historian J.A.R. Marriott, 1932.*

Can these thieves really be our rulers? These thieves… import a huge number of goods made in their own country and sell them in our markets, stealing our wealth and taking life from our people. Can those who steal the harvest of our fields and doom us to hunger, fever and plague really be our rulers? Can foreigners really be our rulers?

↰ **SOURCE C:** *From a leaflet written by Indians who wanted the British out. Who do you think the thieves were?*

Towards independence

By 1900, many educated Indians started to believe that India should be free from British control. A political group called the Indian National Congress was formed to bring this about, but despite holding meetings and organizing demonstrations, the British ignored their demands.

In 1914, Indians fought alongside British soldiers in the Great War (see Source D). India itself gave Britain a huge amount of money, food and materials – and nearly 50,000 Indian soldiers died in the trenches!

In 1919, the British government made slight changes to the way India was governed. Law-making councils were set up in each province and over five million wealthy Indians were given the vote. However, the British government, based in London, still controlled taxation, the police, the law courts, the armed forces, education and much more. Whilst some Indians welcomed the changes as a step in the right direction, others were bitterly disappointed. A demonstration was organized in the town of Amritsar in the province of Punjab and the local British commander ordered his men to fire into the crowd – killing 379 Indian men, women and children.

The Amritsar incident was a turning point for the Indian National Congress and its leader, Mohandas Gandhi. He wrote, 'When a government takes up arms against its unarmed subjects, then it has lost its right to govern.' The Congress, more loudly than ever, demanded an independent India.

⌐ **SOURCE D:** *A picture of Naik Darwan Singh Negi, the first Indian winner of the Victoria Cross, Britain's top bravery medal, in 1914. He was part of an Indian battalion fighting as part of the British Army during the Great War.*

Gandhi

Gandhi, a holy man and a very clever politician, told Indians to do all they could to make life difficult for the British, without using violence. Today, this is called passive resistance. Gandhi called it 'satyagraha', which means 'soul force'. He encouraged strikes, demonstrations and boycotts. His most famous protest occurred in 1930 when he began a campaign against the salt tax. At the time, Indians were not allowed to make their own salt – they had to buy it – and it was heavily taxed by the British government. Gandhi led thousands of Indians to the coast where they began making salt from seawater. All over India, Indians copied Gandhi's example until, after putting 100,000 people in prison, the British gave in and got rid of the salt tax.

By 1935, after many years of protests, the Government of India Act gave Indians the right to control everything except the army. India, however, was still part of the British Empire and was still ruled by a viceroy. Many Indians, including Gandhi, continued to demand complete independence.

⌐ **SOURCE E:** *A photograph of Gandhi, taken in 1925. Every day he span cotton on a small spinning wheel to encourage people to lead simple lives. He wanted Indians to be proud of their country and realize that they didn't need British rule.*

India at war again!

In 1939, when World War Two began, India was still part of the British Empire. As in World War One, thousands of Indians joined up to fight as part of the British Empire force. In total, 2.5 million Indians fought in what was the largest volunteer army in history.

After the war, it was clear that Britain would have to give India its independence. Britain wasn't strong enough to hold on to a country so desperate to rule itself – and the people in Britain, tired of war, weren't keen to see their soldiers trying to control marches and demonstrations that could easily turn to violence.

But the whole matter of independence was complicated by the increasing violence between Hindus and Muslims. Relations had been bad for a long time, but after 1945 they started to break down completely. If India gained its independence, Muslims didn't want to be ruled by a mainly Hindu government (there were a lot more Hindus in India than Muslims). Instead, Muslims wanted a country of their own, made from areas where people were Muslims. They wanted to name this new country after these areas – P for Punjab, A for Afghanis, K for Kashmir, S for Sind and TAN for Baluchistan. The word PAKISTAN also means 'land of the pure' in Urdu.

As violence between Muslims and Hindus continued, the British hurriedly made plans to split India into two countries – India would be for Hindus and Pakistan would be for Muslims. The millions of Sikhs, who felt they didn't belong in either, would have to choose one or the other.

SOURCE F: *Indian soldiers with captured German artillery in the Libyan desert in 1943.*

'How can you even dream of Hindu-Muslim unity? Everything pulls us apart. We have no inter-marriages. We do not have the same calendar. The Muslims believe in a single God, the Hindus worship idols... The Hindus worship animals and consider cows sacred. We, the Muslims, think it is nonsense. We want to kill the cows and eat them. There are only two links between the Muslims and Hindus: British rule – and the common desire to get rid of it.'

SOURCE G: *From a 1944 interview with Mohammed Ali Jinnah, the leader of an Indian political party called the Muslim League. He eventually became Pakistan's first leader.*

Partition of 1947

On 15 August 1947, Britain stopped ruling India. The whole subcontinent was divided into Hindu India and Muslim Pakistan (itself divided into two parts – see Source H). Immediately there were problems. As it was impossible to make sure that boundaries were drawn so that all Muslims were in Pakistan and all Hindus were in India, millions now found themselves in the wrong country. As they fled across the boundaries to be in the country of their religion, whole trainloads were massacred by the 'other side'. Nobody knows exactly how many were killed, but some have estimated as many as one million! Then, at the height of this violence, Gandhi himself, the man who had believed in peaceful protest, was assassinated by an extremist Hindu.

Sadly, the troubled start for the new, independent nations of India and Pakistan continued. Major differences continue to this day.

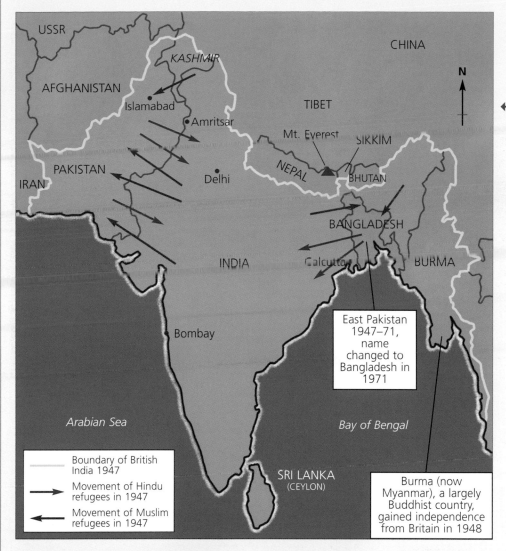

Map labels:
USSR, CHINA, KASHMIR, AFGHANISTAN, Islamabad, Amritsar, TIBET, Mt. Everest, SIKKIM, NEPAL, BHUTAN, PAKISTAN, Delhi, IRAN, BANGLADESH, INDIA, Calcutta, BURMA, Bombay

East Pakistan 1947–71, name changed to Bangladesh in 1971

Arabian Sea

Bay of Bengal

SRI LANKA (CEYLON)

Burma (now Myanmar), a largely Buddhist country, gained independence from Britain in 1948

N

Legend:
— Boundary of British India 1947
→ Movement of Hindu refugees in 1947
← Movement of Muslim refugees in 1947

WISE-UP Words

partition

↵ **SOURCE H:** *How India was divided. Areas where more than half the people were Muslim became Pakistan whilst areas where over half the population were Hindu became India. It has been estimated that over 14 million fled to the 'other side' in 1947. Thousands from both religions were slaughtered on the way.*

Work

1 How do we know that Queen Victoria was proud and pleased about Britain's connection to India?

2 Describe two opposing views of the impact of British rule in India. Why do you think there is such a difference in opinion over this issue?

3 a How did India contribute to the Great War?
  b What changes were made to the way India was governed after the Great War?
  c Why were some Indians happy with these changes? Why were others disappointed?
  d What happened in Amritsar in 1919?

4 a Write a sentence or two about:
   • satyagraha   • salt tax
   • Government of India Act.
  b Can you write a paragraph to link the three together?

5 a Why was India split into two countries in 1947?
  b Why did violence continue even after the split?
  c Look at Source G. In your own words, explain why Jinnah thought unity between Hindus and Muslims was impossible.

MISSION ACCOMPLISHED?

• Would you be able to create a timeline of events charting the gradual movement towards independence that took place in India up to 1947?

↵ **SOURCE I:** *Nehru and Jinnah, the first leaders of the new, independent India and Pakistan.*

! FACT The Empire comes home

As a result of the violence of 1947, many sought safety in the former 'mother country' – Britain. By 1955, there were around 10,000 immigrants from the newly created nations of India, Pakistan and Bangladesh living in Britain. By 1991 around 1.5 million people from the Indian subcontinent were living and working in Britain.

Have you been learning? 1

TASK 1 A different view

Look carefully at the two sources below. Both were written about the impact of the British in India.

SOURCE A

'Ceylon (now Sri Lanka) was unified under British rule in 1815. Over the next 80 years, the British built 2300 miles of road and 2900 miles of railway in India. The land used for farming increased from 400,000 acres to 3.2 million acres, the schools from 170 to 2900, the hospitals from 0 to 65…'

SOURCE B

'Can these thieves really be our rulers? These thieves… import a huge number of goods made in their own country and sell them in our markets, stealing our wealth and taking life from our people. Can those who steal the harvest of our fields and doom us to hunger, fever and plague really be our rulers? Can foreigners really be our rulers?'

a In your own words, try to write a brief summary of what each source says. You will need to re-read each source carefully and sum up the point that each writer is trying to make.

b Which source was written by someone who believes that Britain brought advantages to India? Explain your answer.

c Which source is negative about the British impact on India?

d Can you think of possible reasons why the two sources give such different views about the impact of the British in India?

TASK 2 Making notes

Making notes is an important skill for a historian. To do it successfully, you must pick out all the key words in the sentences. The key words are the pieces of factual information that are vital to the sentences – and without these key words the sentence makes no real sense at all!

For example, in these sentences…

'In 1485, Henry VII was crowned King of England. In 1496 he asked a very famous Italian explorer named John Cabot to go and search for new land around the world.'

… the key words are:

1485; Henry VII; King of England; 1496; asked Italian explorer, John Cabot; look for new land.

Note: The original sentences contain 31 words but there are only 16 key words – yet these notes still allow you to understand the information given in the paragraph!

Now write down the key words in the following sentences. These key words form your notes on the topic!

a In 1492 Christopher Columbus, an Italian explorer working for the Spanish, landed in the Caribbean and claimed several of the islands he found for Spain. He later made three more voyages across the Atlantic and during one of them he landed in South America.

b In 1497 John Cabot, an Italian explorer working for King Henry VII, set sail from Bristol looking for new land to claim for the English King. On 24 June 1497 Cabot saw the coast of North America and claimed it for England. He called it 'New Founde Lande', which eventually became known as Newfoundland in what we now call Canada.

c Eventually, in 1583, an Englishman named Sir Humphrey Gilbert decided to try and set up a colony in Newfoundland. Dozens of English settlers went over to live there, but the colony failed.

d A year later, in 1584, Sir Walter Raleigh was given permission by Queen Elizabeth I to set up another colony further down the North American coast. He named it Virginia after a name Queen Elizabeth was known by – the Virgin Queen.

e However, just like the settlement in Newfoundland, the new Virginia colony failed. A third settlement, which was built in 1587, came to an end when all the settlers mysteriously disappeared. It became known as 'the Lost Colony'.

f Yet another group of settlers tried again in 1607. Their settlement was named Jamestown after the new King of England and Scotland, James. Life there was very tough, but the settlers managed to survive. They began to grow tobacco, which made lots of money. Soon more people began to move to Jamestown, and it looked as if the British in North America were there to stay!

TASK 3 Mapping the world

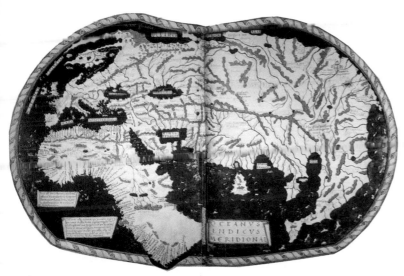

↥ **SOURCE A:** *Map of the world drawn by Henricus Martellus in 1489.*

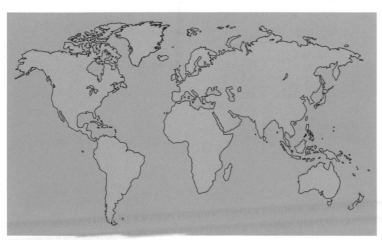

↳ **SOURCE B:** *A modern world map.*

a What major continents and oceans featured on the modern world map are not found on the Martellus map of 1489? You might need to use an Atlas to help you.

b Why do you think these major continents and oceans are not found on the older map?

c Look at the outline of Africa on the older map. Why do you think there are so many place names along the northern and western coasts of Africa, but hardly any on the eastern coast?

d Write a sentence or two about how the following people each helped Europeans learn more about the real size and shape of the world:
- Christopher Columbus
- John Cabot
- Sir Francis Drake
- Vasco da Gama
- Bartholomew Diaz

TASK 4 A slave sale

This is based on an old poster from the USA advertising a 'slave auction'. Use the poster and your own knowledge to answer the following questions.

> **TO BE SOLD AND LET**
> **BY PUBLIC AUCTION**
> *ON SATURDAY 11th MARCH*
> IN THE WEST MEADOW
> ------------------------------
> **FOR SALE,**
> **THE THREE FOLLOWING**
> ## SLAVES
> HANNIBAL, about 30 Years old, an excellent House Servant, of Good Character.
> WILLIAM, about 35 Years old, a Labourer.
> NANCY, an excellent House Servant and Nurse.
> ------------------------------
> **TO BE LET,**
> On the usual conditions of the Hirer finding them in Food, Clothing and Medical Attendance,
> THE FOLLOWING
> **MALE and FEMALE**
> ## SLAVES
> *ROBERT BAGLEY, about 20 Years old, a good House Servant*
> *WILLIAM BAGLEY, about 18 Years old, a Labourer*
> *JOHN ARMS, about 18 Years old*
> *JACK ANTONIA, about 40 Years old, a Labourer*
> *PHILIP, an excellent fisherman*
> *HARRY, about 27 Years old, a good House Servant*
> *LUCY, a Young Woman of good Character, used to House Work and the Nursery*
> *ELIZA, an Excellent Washerwoman*
> *CLARA, an Excellent Washerwoman*
> *HANNAH, about 14 Years old, House Servant*
> *SARAH, about 11 Years old, House Servant*
> ------------------------------
> **Also for Sale, at Eleven o'Clock,**
> **Fine Rice, Books, Muslins, Needles, Pins, Ribbons**

a How many slaves were up for sale in this auction?

b What do you think 'to be let' meant?

c What would the hirer of a slave 'to be let' be expected to provide for them?

d Which of the slaves up for sale would you expect to fetch the highest price? Give reasons for your choice.

e Look at what else is for sale at this auction. What does this tell you about attitudes towards slavery at this time?

f Why were slaves used in North America at this time? You may need to refresh your memory by re-reading pages 18 and 19.

g How did Britain's involvement in the slave trade end? You may need to refresh your memory by re-reading pages 22–25.

So how big was the British Empire?

─────── **MISSION OBJECTIVES** ───────

• To understand what is meant by the term 'the Empire on which the Sun never sets'.

Look at the two maps in Source A. As you can see, in the 1760s (around 250 years ago) the British Empire was quite small. Part of Canada, the American colonies and the islands in the Caribbean were the largest parts of the Empire, whilst the small red dots (mainly in Africa, India and Indonesia) show where British companies had set up trading posts.

Getting bigger

From these beginnings, the British Empire grew and grew. Sometimes the British Government took over the areas where companies went to trade (this happened in Africa and India) – but occasionally the Empire grew as a result of war (this happened in Canada and the West Indies, when Britain took land from France). Perhaps the war seemed defensive when it started, but it nearly always ended up making the Empire even bigger!

By 1924 (the year that the Empire was at its height), the British Empire was huge – the largest in history. It contained around 450 million people, approximately one-quarter of the world's population. And it covered over 14 million square miles, about one-quarter of the Earth's total land area.

⤴ SOURCE A: *The growth of the British Empire in the years from 1765 to 1900.* ⤵

Key

British Empire in 1765

Key

British Empire in 1900

A mixed bag

The Empire was a muddle of different languages, cultures, religions and forms of government. India, for example, contained 300 million people following at least five major religions and speaking at least 15 different languages! Some areas, like Australia, Canada and South Africa, were mainly left to run their own affairs. Other areas, such as India and Egypt, were hugely under British influence – and even had British soldiers based directly in the country.

The whole Empire was run from the Colonial Office in London, set up in 1801. From there, governors, district officers, secretaries and clerks were sent all over the place to govern and administer the Empire.

↵ **SOURCE B:** *The Colonial Office was set up to organize, supervise and manage the colonies of the British Empire. The same building is today home to the Foreign Office.*

The Sun never sets

By the late 1800s some people were beginning to give the British Empire a very famous label – they were calling it 'the Empire on which the Sun never sets'. Put simply, this meant that there were so many countries in the Empire that at any given time of the day or night, there was some place in the Empire where the Sun was shining (see Source C).

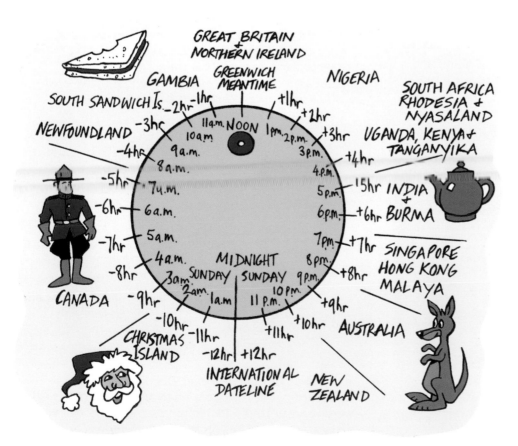

⌐ **SOURCE C:** *The Empire on which the Sun never sets.*

Work ⌐⌐⌐.

1 Explain how each of the following caused the British Empire to grow:
   a trade
   b war.

2 **a** In which year was the British Empire at its largest?
   b Describe the British Empire at this time, making sure you refer to:
   • its size • its population
   • some major countries it ruled.

3 **a** In which year was the Colonial Office set up?
   b What was its purpose?

4 What is meant by the term 'the Empire on which the Sun never sets'? Explain in your own words. You may want to draw your own version of Source C to help you.

─MISSION ACCOMPLISHED?─

• In your own words, can you explain why you think the British Empire was labelled 'the Empire upon which the Sun never sets'?

What did the Empire do for Britain?

―――――――――――――― MISSION OBJECTIVES ――――――――――――――
• To understand at least three ways in which the Empire benefitted Britain.

The most obvious benefit that the British Empire brought to Britain was the opportunity to make money… lots and lots of money! British businessmen, merchants and traders used the Empire to build up personal fortunes, making many of them some of the richest people in the world (see Source A).

There were two main ways for Brits to make money from the Empire:

• Buy (or take) goods from abroad (like sugar, tea, coffee, silk, tobacco and spices) that were hard to get in Britain… and sell them for a high price back home! These goods were extremely popular in the days of the Empire (they still are!) and Britain's citizens were prepared to pay big money to smoke, drink, eat or wear them.

• Buy raw materials abroad very cheaply (like cotton and rubber), make them into goods like clothes and tyres in Britain… and then sell these back to countries in the Empire. This also created jobs for workers in Britain. In fact, by the 1830s most of the cotton worn by Indians was *grown* in India, *made* into clothing in Britain, and then *sold* back to Indians! As a result, Brits got jobs and Brits got rich!

⤷ **SOURCE A:** *This beautiful country house was built in Gloucestershire in 1805. It was paid for by Sir Charles Cockerell, who retired to Britain after making a fortune in India. It was built in an Indian style and was full of furniture brought back from India.*

⤷ **SOURCE B:** *Tea from India being unloaded in the East India Docks in London. In the mid 1800s, the tea trade alone was worth £30 million a year! Trading in goods such as tea, coffee and tobacco not only made money for the traders, but created jobs in shipping, transportation and sales.*

⤷ **SOURCE C:** *Queen Victoria's Diamond Jubilee Celebration, 1897. People from all over the Empire were represented – Indian princes, soldiers from every colony and policemen from Nigeria, Canada and Hong Kong. Never before had Brits seen such evidence of the size of the Empire – and the variety of people within it!*

But the Empire wasn't *just* about making money, there were other benefits too. Read through Source D, which summarizes what else the Empire did for Britain.

Opportunities abroad

For poorer Brits, the Empire became one way to escape unemployment and poor living conditions in Britain. Between 1800 and 1914 about 14 million people emigrated from Britain, mainly to Canada, Australia and New Zealand.

Power

By 1900 Britain ruled about 450 million people living in over 50 colonies around the world. This meant that Britain had plenty of places to keep its warships – and millions of men to call on if it got involved in wars. Indeed, in both World Wars around 40% of the men fighting for Britain were from the Empire.

Work

1 Explain how a British person in the 1800s might have made money from the Empire.

2 Look at Source A. Why do you think Sir Charles Cockerell built his house in this style? What do you think local people thought about it?

3 Imagine you have to explain what the British Empire did for Britain to a primary school student. Produce a poster, leaflet, diagram or PowerPoint® presentation.

Preventing disease

One of the lesser known benefits of the Empire was the contribution it made to fighting diseases like cholera, typhoid and dysentery. These are caused by dirty water – so the rise in tea and coffee drinking helped reduce them! These new drinks introduced from the Empire used boiling water, so the bacteria that caused the diseases were killed.

↖ **SOURCE D:** *So what else did the Empire do for Britain?*

Buildings

What Britain actually looked like changed during the era of empire. The Royal Pavilion in Brighton (see below) is perhaps the best known British building that shows the influence of the Empire – but hundreds of theatres, cinemas, bandstands, kiosks and piers were built in the eighteenth and nineteenth centuries that also reflect a variety of 'Empire styles'. Many of these buildings still exist today (see Source A).

Pride

When Britain first started building its Empire, ordinary Brits were not particularly interested! But by the late 1800s and early 1900s, it was a different story. Brits became more and more proud of the British Empire and this was reflected in the popularity of songs such as 'Rule Britannia' and 'Land of Hope and Glory' – as well as events such as The Festival of the Empire (1911) and the Empire Games (now the Commonwealth Games).

MISSION ACCOMPLISHED?

• Can you remember at least three benefits the British Empire brought to Britain?

A LAND DOWN UNDER

Until the 1700s the Pacific Ocean remained almost unexplored by Europeans. It was a vast area – in fact, the Ocean itself covers an area larger than the continents of North America, South America, Asia and Africa combined! However, European explorers were convinced that a huge area of land existed somewhere in the Pacific Ocean. They even gave it a name, '*Terra Australis Incognita*', which translates as 'unknown southern land'. (Can you see where the name 'Australia' came from?) This Depth Study tells the story of the search for this unknown southern land – and, when land was found, how the Brits came to dominate the area and include it in the British Empire.

1: Finding Australia

—————— MISSION OBJECTIVES ——————
• To explain how European explorers 'found' Australia and New Zealand.

The little cottage pictured in Source A was originally built over 250 years ago in the village of Great Ayton in Yorkshire, England. It was owned by James Cook, a farm worker, who lived there with his family. However, the house is no longer in England – in 1934 it was moved, brick by brick, across to the other side of the world and rebuilt in Australia. Today it is one of the country's top tourist attractions!

So what makes the house so special? Who on earth are the Cook family? And why are Australians so interested in them?

The Cook connection

James Cook (originally from Scotland) and his wife Grace had eight children. The second eldest was also called James and was born in 1728. After five years at school, young James began to work on the farm with his dad, but at 16 he moved to work in a grocer's shop. Bored with this, he soon got a job on a ship carrying coal up and down the English coast. Over the next few years, James sailed all over Europe. He also studied maths, navigation, geometry, map-making and astronomy – all the skills he hoped he'd need one day if he ever commanded his own ship.

In 1755, Cook joined the Royal Navy and was soon promoted… and promoted… and promoted up the ranks. By 1757, Cook was a 'Ship's Master', which meant he was qualified to navigate and handle a ship. He'd also got himself a reputation as a great map-maker.

↵ SOURCE A: *'Cook's Cottage', which was shipped over to Australia in 1934. It was taken over by ship in 253 crates complete with an ivy cutting that had grown on the original building. Today the cottage is covered in the ivy.*

A new voyage

In 1768, after a brilliant career in the Royal Navy, Cook was asked by the Royal Society (a world-famous scientific organization) to captain a ship called 'Endeavour' on a voyage of discovery. His orders were to take a group of scientists, astronomers, **botanists** and artists to explore the Pacific Ocean. He was also asked to look for a great southern continent – the mysterious 'Terra Australis Incognita' or 'unknown southern land'. Explorers knew there was land there somewhere – and had even landed on the west coast of Australia – but they didn't know quite how much land there was, and it had never been mapped properly or 'claimed' by any country!

Land ahoy!

After several months at sea, Cook arrived in New Zealand in 1769 and sailed all around it – making maps as he went. Then, in April 1770, Cook landed on the east coast of Australia at Botany Bay. The area reminded him of South Wales in Britain so he called the whole area New South Wales. This part of Australia is still called New South Wales today! Cook planted a British flag on an island nearby and claimed the territory for Britain… despite the fact that there were native tribes already living in the area. It looked as if Captain Cook had added another huge area of land to the fast-growing British Empire.

★ WISE-UP Words

**Aboriginal Australians
botanists**

! FACT It's ours!
European countries didn't care that the land they 'discovered' was already occupied by people who had lived there for thousands of years. As far as the Europeans were concerned, they had the power (i.e. the guns) and the right (they were Christians and these 'natives' weren't) to take all the land they wanted. In fact, they saw it as their duty to bring Christianity to the 'godless' natives!

⌐ **SOURCE B:** *Captain Cook claims Australia for the British in April 1770. Note his ship, 'Endeavour', in the background.*

The *real* Australians

When Cook arrived in Australia he wrote in his diary that 'when we got near the beach we could see several people of a dark or black colour'. Cook was referring to the native people whose ancestors had lived in Australia for over 40,000 years. These people are sometimes called **Aboriginal Australians** (see Source C).

When Cook first arrived in Australia there were approximately 500,000 Aboriginal Australians living all over Australia, speaking 200 different languages. Generally the tribes lived 'off the land' and moved around to different areas at different times of year hunting for food. Tragically, diseases that the British brought with them to Australia (like smallpox) would kill around half of the Aboriginal Australian population over the next few decades.

⤷ SOURCE C: *One of the first Australians, known today as Aboriginal Australians. Note the boomerang used for hunting. The word 'Aboriginal' has been used by the English since the 1700s. It's from the Latin words 'ab' (meaning 'from') and 'origo' (meaning 'beginning').*

A few years after Cook's first landing, the Brits returned to Australia to set up the first permanent settlement. The colony they built later became the city of Sydney, the largest city in modern-day Australia.

So what happened to Captain Cook?

Captain Cook made two more voyages to explore the Southern Pacific Ocean, even crossing the Antarctic Circle and sailing further south than anyone had sailed before. He wrote in his diary that he had 'put an end to the search for the southern continent'. However, on Cook's final voyage he was killed by local tribesmen soon after landing in Hawaii. It seems that Cook was often tough on natives he met on his voyages – and this perhaps led to his untimely death! What was left of his body was buried at sea on 21 February 1779. Today, the site in Hawaii where Cook was killed is marked by a monument, and the area around it has been given to the United Kingdom! Therefore, the site is officially part of the UK.

⤷ SOURCE D: *Cook's death. He was killed on 14 February 1779 in Hawaii during a quarrel over a stolen boat.*

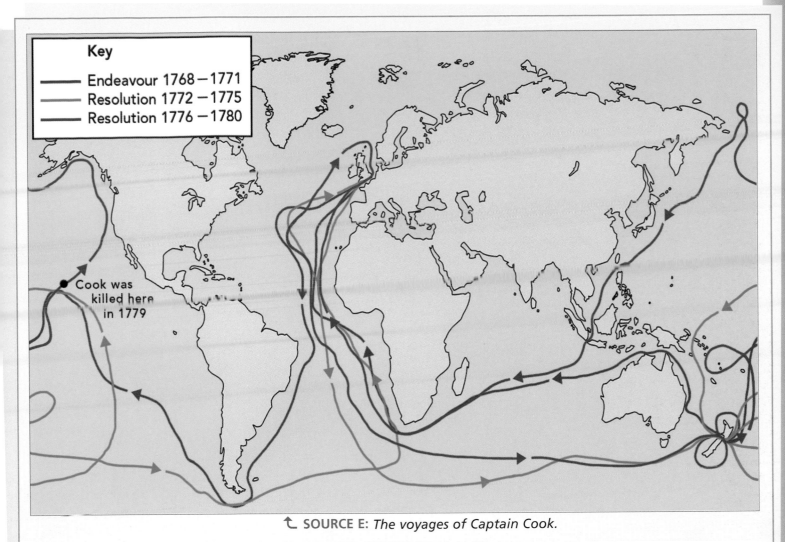

Key
— Endeavour 1768–1771
— Resolution 1772–1775
— Resolution 1776–1780

Cook was killed here in 1779

↳ **SOURCE E:** *The voyages of Captain Cook.*

Captain Cook today

Captain Cook spent over 12 years sailing around the Pacific Ocean. He discovered new places and created incredibly accurate maps. He was regarded as an excellent commander who took good care of his sailors. Australia today is full of places named after him, including a university, a hospital, and numerous schools, towns and landmarks. His image has appeared on banknotes, stamps and coins – and there is even a crater named after him on the Moon!

Amazingly, in 1934 an Australian businessman bought the cottage in England once owned by Captain Cook's parents… and had it shipped, brick by brick, over to Melbourne, Australia. It is unlikely that Captain Cook ever lived in the cottage – but it seems the fact that he probably once visited was enough reason to buy it!

Work

1 a What did the term 'Terra Australis Incognita' mean?
b Can you suggest some reasons why the Terra Australis Incognita remained undiscovered by Europeans for so long?

2 The following dates are all important in the James Cook story: 1755; 1779; 1768; 1770; 1728; 1769; 1757.
Write each date on a separate line in your book, in chronological order. Beside each date, write what happened in that year.

3 a Write down five bullet point facts about Aboriginal Australians.
b What immediate impact did the British have on Aboriginal Australians?

4 Look at Source A.
a What does the photograph show… and where is it?
b Why do you think it was moved to its new place?
c How else is Captain James Cook remembered in Australia today?

MISSION ACCOMPLISHED?

• Can you explain what is meant by the term 'Terra Australis Incognita'?
• Could you discuss why Australians today think the voyages of James Cook are so significant?

When Captain James Cook returned from Australia he reported to the British Government that it would make a good place for a settlement. It didn't matter to the Brits that there were already people living there (the Aboriginal Australians) – because as far as Britain was concerned, the whole country was '*terra nullius*', a legal term meaning 'land belonging to no one'. The Brits thought that because the Aboriginal Australians did not farm the land (like the British did) they were therefore 'uncivilized'.

2: Transportation nation

MISSION OBJECTIVES

• To understand the difference between a 'first fleeter', a 'free settler' and a 'transported convict'.

The 'First Fleet'

The British Government decided to send a well-known naval commander, Captain Arthur Phillip, to set up the first settlement or colony on Australian soil. They also wanted him to take over 700 convicts from Britain's overcrowded jails to help him do it. It was hoped that these prisoners would never return to Britain – after their sentences were completed, they would be forced to stay in Australia because they wouldn't be able to get home!

In May 1787, 11 ships left Portsmouth heading for the new British colony of Australia. There were over 1300 people on board the ships in total, including 736 convicted criminals. These 11 ships are today known in Australia as the 'First Fleet' and are acknowledged as the 'Founders of Australia'. They arrived on 26 January 1788, now known as Australia Day or Foundation Day. In 2004, an estimated 8 million people attended Australia Day celebrations across the country.

↵ **SOURCE A:** *Captain Arthur Phillip inspecting convicts in his new colony, 1788. Captain Phillip became Governor Phillip, the man in charge of Australia's first British colony. Today, all sorts of things are named after him in Australia, including a port, several islands and many streets, parks and schools.*

Life down under

The oldest convict on the First Fleet was an 82-year-old woman called Dorothy Handland. She survived the trip but hanged herself from a tree when she saw the conditions in which she was expected to live. John Hudson, who had stolen some clothes and a gun, was the youngest convict. He was nine years old.

The convicts began to build the settlement. Each convict was assigned a master who used them to carry out whatever work they wanted for the rest of their sentence. This was usually for seven years, fourteen years… or life! Good, hardworking convicts earned themselves an early release, whilst bad behaviour ended in a whipping – or an extended sentence! Over the next 20 years, British courts transported over 20,000 more convicts to join them.

Sources A to C show the colony's early history as a 'transportation nation'.

· James Clay – 16 January 1822 – transported for seven years for stealing mathematics equipment.
· Megan Leach – 29 June 1831 – transported for 14 years for stealing three ducks.
· James Morris – 25 June 1840 – transported for life for stealing various goods from Thomas Dawson.

⤶ **SOURCE B:** *A selection of convict records from Nottingham Borough Courthouse, 1822–1852.*

❚❚ PAUSE for Thought
Some Australians call 26 January 'Invasion Day' – can you think why?

- **Age** – the average age of a convict was 27.
- **Sex** – about 15% of convicts were women.
- **Nationality** – 70% English and Welsh; 25% Irish; 5% Scottish.
- **Crimes** – 80% were thieves; most had been convicted several times. About 5% had committed violent crimes.

⤴ **SOURCE C:** *A typical convict.*

⤴ **SOURCE D:** *The first British colony in Australia in 1800. It was named Sydney after a British politician. Note the Aboriginal Australians looking down on the colony.*

Free settlers

Life in the new settlement was tough. Few of the convicts – or their masters – knew about farming or carpentry, two of the most important skills needed in the new colony. In fact, the new settlement was lucky to survive its early years. However, in 1790 the first 'free settlers' began to arrive from Britain, attracted by the idea of a new life in another part of the world. They brought the supplies and skills needed to help the settlement survive… and grow. More convict ships arrived too and by 1800 the British population in Australia had grown to around 6000. Source D shows the colony around this time.

Brits abroad

Over the next 50 years the Brits began to explore the different parts of Australia. When the explorers returned with reports of what they had seen or found, the settlers began to move inland, hoping to set up farms or look for gold and other valuable gemstones such as opal.

New settlements were set up in Hobart (1803), on the Brisbane River (1824), on the Swan River (1829), on Port Phillip Bay (1835) and on Gulf St. Vincent (1836). By this time, the British population in Australia stood at around 130,000. Today, the huge cities of Hobart (in Tasmania, the island to the south of mainland Australia), Brisbane, Perth, Melbourne and Adelaide are found at these sites!

A new generation

Australia was first used by the Brits mainly as a place to dump their criminals – but things soon started to change. The majority of convicts decided to stay in Australia at the end of their sentences. Many became sheep or wheat farmers. An 'Australia-born' generation grew up too – people who were born in Australia and regarded themselves as 'Australian'. And with more free settlers arriving, the population of Australia grew to 405,000 by 1850. By now the colonies each had their own councils and governors who were starting to make decisions about how to run things. Soon, this new generation of Australians began to object to what they thought of as 'their country' being used as a dumping ground for Britain's criminals. Transportation ended in 1868 – by which time a total of 162,000 convicts had been sent to Australia on 806 'transport ships'.

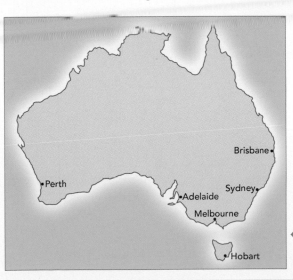

↵ **SOURCE E:** *Cities in modern Australia that grew from the early settlements.*

Work

1. What did the British mean when they declared Australia 'terra nullius'?

2. a What was 'transportation' and why was it introduced?
   b Who were the 'first fleeters' and the 'free settlers'?

3. a The population of settlers in Australia is mentioned four times in this spread – in 1788, 1800, 1836 and 1850. Draw a graph to show how it changed.
   b Why do you think the population grew so much?

—— MISSION ACCOMPLISHED? ——

- In your own words, can you describe how white settlers gradually colonized Australia?

There had been people living in Australia for thousands and thousands of years before the British went to settle there. In fact, the earliest human remains discovered in Australia have been found to be about 40,000 years old. The people who lived in Australia before the Brits arrived are known collectively as 'Aboriginal Australians'.

3: Adventure or invasion?

_____MISSION OBJECTIVES_____

• To know why there was conflict between white settlers and Aboriginal Australians.

Aboriginal Australians lived as **hunter-gatherers**, which means they gathered edible plants and killed wild animals to eat in order to survive. It seems they were **nomadic** too, which means they moved around the countryside to hunt and gather, rather than staying in one place. When the British first arrived in Australia, it has been estimated that there were approximately half a million Aboriginal Australians living in about 200 different groups (or nations), and speaking about 200 different languages.

WISE-UP Words

hunter-gatherers
nomadic

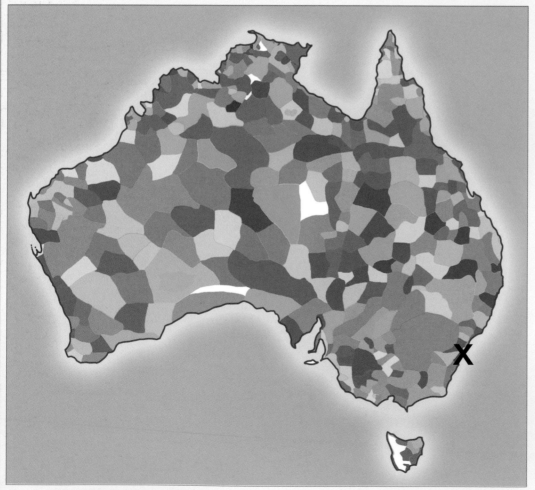

↳ SOURCE A: _The Aboriginal Australian nations before the British arrived. Each colour represents an area where a particular Aboriginal Australian tribe lived. The 'X' marks where Captain Cook landed in April 1770. The first colony was set up nearby in 1788 at Botany Bay._

The largest group, or nation, of Aboriginal Australians living near to where the first British colony was set up in 1788 was the Darug people. Within three years of white settlement, about 90% of the whole nation had been killed, mainly due to diseases brought over by the settlers. As white settlers began to explore more of Australia and settle in new places, they came into direct contact with these 'first Australians' – Aboriginal Australians. Look carefully at the two cartoons on the next page. They show how the expansion of the British Empire in Australia can be interpreted in different ways.

Speech bubbles (British settler, left):

Once again, the British have discovered another part of the world and claimed it for our Empire.

The story of settlement in Australia is one of adventure to an unknown part of the world and a heroic struggle to overcome difficulties in a hostile environment.

No one owns the land here anyway – so it's up for grabs. The tribes that live here can't prove it's theirs – and they don't even farm, mine or build towns like us civilized Brits.

The tribes are not civilized at all. They lead the most basic lives and are not advanced in any way. They need our help.

Speech bubbles (Aboriginal man, right):

This land may be 'undiscovered' to Europeans – but we certainly know it's here! We've been here for thousands of years after all!

The British arrival was an invasion – pure and simple. It was a chance to expand their Empire at the cost of a peaceful nation. We had never threatened the Brits!

We don't live in the same sort of world as the whites – but that doesn't make us backward! We don't have courts and documents to show we own our land – we just share it between ourselves, taking what we need and not being greedy.

We have thrived in this country for years – yet the first white settlers nearly died because they couldn't cope. They only survived because more settlers came to help them!

We are not uncivilized and backward – just different! We have strong traditions that go back centuries. We are deeply spiritual, and wonderful storytellers. We also enjoy art, music and dancing.

Terrorists or freedom fighters?

Many Aboriginal Australians resisted the arrival of white settlers and fought against the Brits who began to farm and mine the land that the tribes had lived on. One of the first leaders of this resistance was Pemulwuy, a member of the Bidjigal nation, who lived near Botany Bay. He organized tribes living in the area to carry out attacks on British settlers and their property. In 1790 he killed one of Governor Phillip's workers, a man he believed had killed four Aboriginal Australians. In retaliation, the British killed several people from Pemulwuy's tribe.

Despite a massive hunt for Pemulwuy and his followers, he avoided capture for 12 years. He was once shot seven times during a battle – but this just added to the rumour that Pemulwuy could not be killed by English guns! Eventually, though, Pemulwuy was shot dead in 1802 during an ambush. His head was cut off and sent to London with a letter saying that he 'was a terrible pest to the colony, but a brave and independent character'.

In Australia today, Pemulwuy is a very famous Aboriginal Australian. There is even an area of Sydney named after him, and a park. Other 'resistance fighters' who led their people against the British settlers, like Yagan and Jandamarra, are well known too, and their stories are taught to Australian school children.

↳ **SOURCE B:** *A painting of the head of Aboriginal freedom fighter Yagan, which was cut off and put on display in a museum in England after he was killed in 1833.*

Hunted like animals

To most white settlers, the Aboriginal Australians were seen as 'the enemy' – and land that their ancestors had lived on for thousands of years was simply taken by force. Tribespeople on foot, armed with spears, were no match for soldiers on horseback with the latest rifles! In some cases, the Aboriginal Australians were hunted and killed like animals – as a sport! (See Sources C, D and E.)

'I have heard again and again people say that they were nothing better than dogs, and it was no more harm to shoot them than it would be to shoot a dog when he barked at you.'

↳ **SOURCE D:** *Reverend William Yate, 1835.*

! FACT Terror in Tasmania
When the British reached the Australian island of Tasmania in 1802, there were 20,000 Aboriginal Australians living there. Eighty years later, there was not a single one left!

The 'Stolen Generations'

In the later part of the 1800s there was an attempt in many areas to strip Aboriginal Australians of their heritage and cultural identity. For example, children were taken from their families to go and live in white Christian homes, and their grief-stricken parents made to work for white settlers. The children were forbidden to speak their own language or take part in their traditional rituals. They had to get special permission to marry when they were older or to move from place to place, and their employment was strictly controlled. These children, perhaps as many as 100,000, who were taken from their families between 1869 and 1969 are known as the 'Stolen Generations'. And in January 2008, the whole of the country stopped to listen as Australia's Prime Minister officially apologized for the treatment of these Aboriginal Australian children (see Source F).

SOURCE F: *Part of the Australian Prime Minister's apology to the Aboriginal Australian children of the 'Stolen Generations'.* ↱

'I count it a fine sport to shoot a native as a kangaroo.'

↳ **SOURCE C:** *A comment from a white settler in Australia.*

↳ **SOURCE E:** *Hunting Aboriginal Australians, a picture from 1860. From 1788 to 1921 it has been estimated that the Aboriginal Australian population dropped by 80%.*

'We apologize for the laws and policies of successive governments that have inflicted profound grief, suffering and loss on these, our fellow Australians.

We apologize especially for the removal of Aboriginal children from their families, communities and their country.

For the pain, suffering and hurt of these Stolen Generations, their descendants and for their families left behind, we say sorry.

To the mothers and the fathers, the brothers and the sisters, for the breaking up of families and communities, we say sorry.

And for the indignity and degradation this inflicted on a proud people and a proud culture, we say sorry'.

Aboriginal Australians today

By 1900 the population of Aboriginal Australians had declined to about 90,000. Today the population stands at around 500,000, making up about 2.5% of Australia's population. Sadly, there are huge differences in such things as life expectancy, education, employment and health when comparing Aboriginal Australians to white Australians (see Source G). Clearly, there is still a long way to go in order to put the descendants of the first Australians on an equal footing with those of the white settlers!

	Aboriginal Australians	White Australians
Life expectancy (men)	67.2 years	78.7 years
Life expectancy (women)	72.9 years	82.6 years
College education	39%	75%
University education	22%	48%
Unemployed	20%	7%

↳ **SOURCE G:** *A comparison between Aboriginal Australians and white Australians in recent years. Recent figures also show that Aboriginal Australians were 11 times more likely to be in prison, and twice as likely to be a victim of violent aggression. Aboriginal Australians earn, on average, 40% less than white Australians.*

SOURCE H: *In recent years, the Aboriginal Australian population has worked hard to get their own flag recognized. It is now on display in some prominent Australian buildings. Black represents the colour of the people, red is the colour of the land and yellow is for the Sun.* ↱

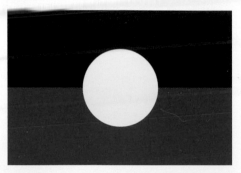

↳ **SOURCE I:** *Cathy Freeman, one of Australia's most famous Aboriginal Australians, draped in both the Australian and Aboriginal flags after winning gold in the women's 400 metres at the 2000 Olympics in Sydney.*

Work

1 In history it is important to understand that there are different points of view.
   a Why did the British think that it was acceptable to build their settlements in Australia, even if it meant conflict with the Aboriginal Australians?
   b Why do you think many Aboriginal Australians resisted the settler 'invasion' so strongly?
   c Suggest why opposing points of view are so common in history.

2 Design a leaflet, poster, mind map or PowerPoint® presentation about the struggle between British settlers and the Aboriginal Australians. Make sure you include:
   • a detailed definition of the term 'Aboriginal Australian'
   • information about the Aboriginal Australian way of life
   • reasons why the settlers and Aboriginal Australians clashed
   • the story of Pemulwuy
   • details of the 'Stolen Generations'
   • facts about Aboriginal Australians today.

—— **MISSION ACCOMPLISHED?** ——

• Can you explain how and why the expansion of the British Empire in Australia can be interpreted in different ways?

The first British settlers (and convicts) arrived in Australia in 1788. They built their first settlement around a harbour, and this later grew into the city of Sydney. More people arrived and began to settle in different parts of Australia over the next few decades. By the 1830s there were lots of different settlements around Australia, and the country itself was divided into four separate 'provinces' – New South Wales, Western Australia, South Australia and the island of Tasmania (see Source A).

4: An independent Australia

MISSION OBJECTIVES

• To know how Australians gradually gained more and more freedom to run their own affairs.

There were special councils in each of the four Australian provinces – with governors in charge – that took some responsibility for running things in the province. The provinces were all run slightly differently, having different rules and ideas about land, education, the railways, and so on. Of course, Australia was still part of the British Empire and all the big decisions were made by the British Parliament – but the everyday running of each province was left to the governor and his council.

However, by 1901 Australia was a united nation, running itself and making key decisions that concerned the *whole* of the country through its own parliament. So how did this change happen? The cartoon shows how an 'independent Australia' came into being.

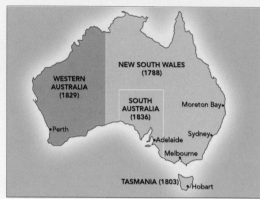

↱ SOURCE A: *The four provinces of Australia in 1836.*

1770: Captain Cook claims Australia for the British.

1788: First colony built in Sydney Cove.

1790: First free settlers arrive for a new life in Australia.

1803: New colony set up for convicts on Tasmania. Free settlers soon follow.

1840: By now, about half the people living in Australia were born there.

1851: Gold discovered in Australia – even more settlers arrive. Population now nearly half a million.

1851: A new province is set up – called Victoria (named after whom?)

1855: Four of the five provinces of Australia granted 'self-government'. They manage most of their own affairs but are still part of the British Empire.

1859: Queensland, the last colony to be created, comes into existence.

1890: By now all six provinces or territories are 'self-governing'.

1891: Now over 80% of people in Australia were born there. The six colonies meet to draw up a set of rules about how to run Australia as a united country, independent of Britain.

1901: The 'Commonwealth of Australia' comes into existence. All the territories form one 'Federation' with its own Parliament. But the British monarch remains the head of state!

Birth of a nation

1901 is a very important year in Australian history. It marks the birth of a nation – that is, when all six independent territories joined as one to form 'Australia'. A new capital city was even built from scratch – Canberra – because they couldn't decide whether it should be Melbourne or Sydney. Soon after, a new flag was created (see Source B).

The new Australia quickly created its own army and navy, as well as new laws on education, transport, pensions and much more. However, there were still some legal links to Britain after 1901. For example, the British Parliament could (if it chose to) meddle with the powers of Australia's Parliament. This never actually happened – but the idea still annoyed Australians. Over the next few decades though, Australia gradually gained more and more control, until finally, in 1986, Australia became totally independent of Britain.

↵ **SOURCE B:** *The Australian flag. A competition was held to choose the new flag. The stars represent the Southern Cross, one of the clearest and best known star constellations seen in Australia.*

Work

1 a List the four Australian provinces or territories that existed by 1836.
  b Why do you think Britain let these areas run certain things themselves?
  c What sort of things did each province control?

2 a List the six Australian provinces or territories that existed by 1859.
  b Which two were named in honour of Queen Victoria?

3 Today, many Australians claim that 1901 marked the 'birth of their nation'. What do you think they mean?

— **MISSION ACCOMPLISHED?** —

• Could you create a timeline charting the history of Australia from 'colonization to independence' (1770–1901)?

Look at the painting in Source A. It shows a very famous event in New Zealand's history – the signing of the Treaty of Waitangi between Maori tribespeople and the British. The tribespeople are agreeing to be ruled by the British, and to sell them their land. In return the Maoris are guaranteed protection and status as British citizens! So how did the Treaty come about? Was it a fair deal? What are the British doing in New Zealand in the first place? And what happened when the British government bought all the Maori land they could – and sold it for huge profits to thousands of British settlers?

5: What about New Zealand?

MISSION OBJECTIVES

- To be able to describe *when*, *why* and *how* the British colonized New Zealand.

First arrivals

The first Maori settlers reached New Zealand about 1000 years ago. They arrived in longboats from their ancient homelands of islands in the Pacific Ocean looking for new places to fish, hunt and grow crops. The Maori tribes lived mainly around the coast in small communities. By the time the first white settlers arrived there were about 100,000 Maoris living all over New Zealand.

! FACT **What's in a name?**
The Maori name for New Zealand was 'Aotearoa', meaning 'Land of the Long White Cloud'.

⌐ **SOURCE A:** *Maori chiefs sign the Treaty of Waitangi in February 1840.*

⌐ **SOURCE B:** *Maori tribesmen dancing a 'Haka' (traditional war dance) in their village in the 1800s. The Haka was meant to invoke the God of War before battle – or simply frighten your enemy away! The Haka is still performed today by several New Zealand sports teams before they compete.*

The Europeans arrive

The first European to find New Zealand was the Dutch explorer Abel Tasman, in 1642. In fact, the Dutch were the ones who named it 'New Zealand' after an area of Holland called Zeeland. Maori tribesmen killed four of Tasman's sailors – and no Europeans returned to New Zealand for over a hundred years.

In 1769 Captain James Cook reached New Zealand and drew maps of the coastline. Over the next few years lots of traders from Europe started going there to trade metal tools and weapons for Maori timber, food and artefacts. Some even settled there – and by 1800 there were about 2000 Pakeha (the Maori word for 'Europeans') living in New Zealand. Many Christian **missionaries** went there too, eager to convert the Maoris to Christianity.

SOURCE C: Early settlers are met by native Maoris in New Zealand, around 1800.

WISE-UP Words

missionaries

A British colony

In the 1830s, French traders began visiting New Zealand more and more. The British thought they were about to claim it for France – so quickly sent an army to claim it for Britain instead! In 1840 the British hurriedly wrote up the Treaty of Waitangi – and asked Maori chiefs to sign it (see Source A). The Treaty said that the tribes that had lived in New Zealand for hundreds of years were now Brits – and had agreed to sell their land to Britain. In short, New Zealand had become a new British colony.

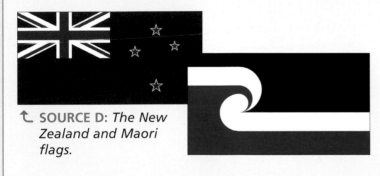

⌐ SOURCE D: The New Zealand and Maori flags.

A fair deal?

Before the British arrived the Maoris had no idea that people could own land. They saw themselves as guardians of the land, which belonged to everyone. It is unlikely that the Maoris would have agreed to the deal if they had fully understood what would happen!

As soon as the Treaty was signed, the British government bought as much land as they could as cheaply as possible. They then resold the land to new settlers for huge profits, and the settlers divided it up and fenced it off. By 1855 the white population had grown to about 200,000 and conflict over land between Maoris and the settlers led to war… which resulted in the loss of more Maori land, as well as the deaths of many Maori warriors.

The settlers in control

In 1856 the British government allowed New Zealand to become 'self-governing'. This meant that the settlers could vote for their own politicians to represent them in their own Parliament. The Maoris could vote too (they were British citizens, remember!), although many chose not to! In 1893, the country became the first in the world to grant women the right to vote… and by the 1900s New Zealand was fully independent of Britain. However, New Zealand did fight on Britain's side in both World Wars and links between the two nations remain close.

So what about the Maoris?

By 1900 there were only about 35,000 Maoris left living on some of the poorest land. There were over 750,000 white New Zealanders by then! Gradually, though, Maori numbers started to increase again and there are now over 600,000 people of Maori descent in New Zealand, out of a population of just over 4,000,000. In the twentieth century some Maori tribes began to take legal action to get compensation for the land they lost in the 1800s. The largest settlement, in June 2008, saw the New Zealand government transfer nine huge areas of valuable farmland back to Maori tribes.

! FACT How close?
New Zealand is 1250 miles away from Australia – a lot further than most people think. This is about the same distance from London… to the African coast!

Work

1 Look at the following dates:
   • 1769 • 1642 • 1856 • 1840 • 2008 • 1893.

   Write down the dates in order and explain why each is significant in the history of New Zealand.

2 a Explain what was agreed in the Treaty of Waitangi.

   b What is your opinion of the Treaty? Was it fair? Did the Maoris get a good deal or not?

___ **MISSION ACCOMPLISHED?** ___

• Can you explain key terms such as Aotearoa, Maori, Pakeha and Haka?

Did the Empire strike back?

MISSION OBJECTIVES

• To remember at least three ways in which the British faced defeat during the era of empire.

The Brits spent many years conquering countries all over the world and making them part of the largest Empire the world had ever seen. But don't be fooled into thinking that the people in the areas the Brits conquered were happy about the invasion of their land. Far from it. On many occasions they fiercely resisted the British soldiers and settlers who came to colonize the area. Read through the information below carefully – it outlines several instances of the Empire fighting back!

The Maroons

The Maroons (from the Spanish *cimarrones*, meaning 'living on mountain top') were runaway slaves who lived in the West Indies, mainly on the British-run Caribbean island of Jamaica. They controlled large areas of the central part of the island and often raided the British plantations to take food and supplies. They were highly organized and skilled hunters – and, hard as they tried, the British Army could not control or defeat them. Eventually, the Brits made a peace deal with the Maroons – and employed them to hunt down other escaped slaves!

THE INDIA & COLONIAL EXHIBITION.
LONDON, 1886.
MAP OF THE WORLD
SHEWING THE EXTENT OF THE
BRITISH EMPIRE IN 1886.

British Territories Coloured Solid Blue, and also as this

↵ **SOURCE A:** *A painting of Chief Hone Heke chopping down the flagpole in 1845. Although the Brits remained in control, the fact that the flagpole was not re-erected after it was cut down for the final time was seen as a great victory for Hone Heke.*

The Flagpole War

In the 1800s New Zealand became part of the British Empire. Any Maori who resisted the takeover felt the full force of the British Army. However, in 1845 one rebel Maori leader came up with a novel way to annoy them! As a sign of his unhappiness, Chief Hone Heke chopped down the flagpole carrying the British flag that flew over the British fort near his homeland. And when the Brits replaced it, he did it again. And again. Dozens of British soldiers were killed trying to defend the flagpole too! Eventually, after many battles, a ceasefire was agreed… but the flagpole stayed down!

Easter Rising

In the Middle Ages, Ireland was an independent Catholic nation. But in the 1600s and 1700s, English and Scottish Protestants began to settle there – and took lots of Irish land. In 1801, Ireland became part of the United Kingdom run by Parliament in London. Many Irish people didn't like this – they were mainly Catholics and were called Nationalists. However, there were other Irish people who did want to be part of the United Kingdom, mainly Protestants in the northern part of Ireland called Ulster. They were called Unionists.

At Easter 1916, a group of Nationalists seized various buildings in Dublin and proclaimed Irish independence. The Brits sent in troops to sort out the rebels and within a week the Easter Rising had been stopped. Hundreds of Irish civilians were killed and 15 of the rebel leaders were shot. These men were seen as national heroes – and it made many Irish people more determined to fight for independence. In the years after the Easter Rising there was much violence between Nationalists and Unionists. Eventually, in July 1921, a solution was proposed. The 26 counties of southern Ireland would become a dominion within the British Empire known as the Irish Free State, and would run their own affairs. The other part of Ireland (Northern Ireland) would remain part of the UK.

By 1949 the Irish Free State had changed its name to Eire (Southern Ireland) and was completely separate from the British Empire. Northern Ireland was (and still is) part of the UK.

⬑ SOURCE B: *Ireland after it was divided.*

↵ SOURCE C: *Chinese soldiers, who had been helping the international forces fight the Boxers, pictured standing over the executed bodies of four Boxer Rebels.*

The Boxer Rebellion

In China there was a group called the 'Society of Righteous Fists' (or 'Boxers'). They believed that their strange boxing exercises protected them from harm. The Boxers were fed up with foreigners interfering in China and taking land. They were unhappy with the Brits, for example, because they had been selling opium (an addictive drug) in China for years, and when the Chinese objected, war had broken out (the Opium Wars). The Brits beat the Chinese and took even more land, including Hong Kong!

In 1898, groups of Boxers began to roam China, killing any Chinese people who had converted to Christianity (a foreign religion) and destroying foreign churches, railway lines and warehouses. However, after months of attacks, an international army of around 50,000 from Russia, Japan, France, Germany, Italy and Britain arrived in China and finally defeated the Boxers.

The Afghan disaster

In 1838 a British army of around 16,000 went to Afghanistan (next to India) to increase Britain's grip on the region. Although they managed to capture the capital, Kabul, and put their own man in charge, the Afghans fought back ferociously. They killed the top British general – and paraded his chopped-up body through the streets. In 1842 the Brits decided to leave, but were attacked again and again as they marched back towards India. Of the 16,000 that set out on the return journey, only one man – William Brydon – made it back to the British base!

Work

1 Write a sentence or two to explain who the following were:
   • The Maroons
   • Chief Hone Heke   • The Boxers.

2 In your own words explain *how* and *why* different groups fought back against the British in the following areas:
   a The West Indies
   b Afghanistan
   c New Zealand
   d Ireland
   e China.

3 Why do you think the British usually dealt harshly with rebellions like these?

—MISSION ACCOMPLISHED?—

• Can you provide details of three examples of British defeats during the era of Empire?

Did the Empire help win two World Wars?

—————————— MISSION OBJECTIVES ——————————
• To understand how troops from all over the British Empire contributed to the war effort during World Wars One and Two.

Meet two very brave men. So brave that they were both awarded top bravery medals by the British government. The soldier on the left is Khudadad Khan and he won a Victoria Cross (VC) fighting for the British in World War One. The VC is Britain's highest honour that any soldier can win! The man on the right is Ulric Cross, a navigator on a British bomber plane during World War Two. He won a Distinguished Flying Cross (DFC) and a Distinguished Service Order (DSO), two of the Royal Air Force's top awards. Neither was born in Britain – or had even been there until the wars started – but they were still prepared to risk their lives fighting for Britain. So why did men like Khudadad and Ulric join up to fight? What contribution did the 'soldiers of empire' make to the war effort? Indeed, did the Empire help Britain win two World Wars?

↱ **SOURCE A:** *Khudadad Khan, pictured in the Daily Mirror in 1915. Born in what is now Pakistan, Khan won his VC in October 1914 after he was wounded, fought off a German attack with only his rifle, and managed to get back to the trenches after being left for dead.*

↱ **SOURCE B:** *Ulric Cross was one of 250 Trinidadians who joined the RAF when World War Two broke out. He flew over 80 bombing missions, 20 of them over Germany. His plane landed seven times without its wheels because they had been shot away or wouldn't lower!*

SOURCE C: *A World War One recruitment poster, sent out to the colonies of the British Empire. Posters sent to India promised 'an easy life', 'good pay' and 'very little danger'! The posters clearly did the trick – by December 1914, one in every three soldiers fighting for Britain in France was from India.* ↱

'Soldiers of empire' during World War One

When World War One broke out in 1914 there was a great rush of young men volunteering in Britain to fight 'for King and Country'. But there was a huge wave of enthusiasm in the Empire too, as thousands of Indians, Canadians, New Zealanders, South Africans, Australians and West Indians decided to 'do their bit' as well. This was lucky for Britain, because when war broke out there were ten times as many soldiers in the German Army as there were in the British Army. The British government had no choice but to use the Empire soldiers.

THE EMPIRE NEEDS MEN!

THE OVERSEAS STATES
All answer the call.
Helped by the YOUNG LIONS
The OLD LION defies his foes.
ENLIST NOW.

The number of Empire soldiers fighting in World War One was huge. For example, Canada sent nearly half a million men, Australia sent over 300,000 and New Zealand sent nearly 130,000 – about one-tenth of the entire population of the country. About 200,000 Irishmen served in the British forces too, and India sent around 1.4 million soldiers!

> 'When Britain is at war, Canada is at war – there is no difference at all.'

↳ **SOURCE D:** *The Prime Minister of Canada in October 1914.*

SOURCE E: *An Australian recruitment poster. The Australians and New Zealanders (known as the ANZacs) fought in some of the toughest fighting of all in World War One – against the Turks in the Gallipoli Campaign, for example.* ↱

↳ **SOURCE F:** *The British West Indies Regiment in 1916. West Indian troops were usually used as ammunition carriers (a very dangerous job), rather than fighting soldiers. Some were unhappy with the 'lack of action' – and many were treated badly whilst in France. One Trinidadian sergeant wrote: 'We are treated neither as Christians nor British citizens, but as West Indian "niggers", without anyone to be interested in or look after us.'*

At the end of World War One, Britain's war dead numbered over 700,000 – and the Empire combined had lost over 200,000 men. For example, India lost 64,000 soldiers, Australia and New Zealand lost 67,000 and Canada lost 56,000. And Empire troops were involved in some of the bloodiest campaigns and battles of the entire war – Ypres, the Somme, Gallipoli and Passchendaele. Empire troops also won hundreds of medals during the war, including over 150 Victoria Crosses – the highest bravery award in the British Empire!

Work

1 a Who were Khudadad Khan and Ulric Cross? Give at least three facts about each of them.
b Can you think of reasons why men like Khudadad and Ulric might have joined up to fight for the British?

2 Look at Source C. Write a sentence or two explaining:
- who the poster was meant to appeal to
- how it tried to do this
- how successful you think it was in getting men to fight.

3 Look at Source F and read the caption carefully.
a What sort of job did these men do in the war?
b How were they treated according to the sergeant quoted?
c Can you think of reasons why they were treated this way?

> 'The Indians have overwhelmed the British nation by their complete enthusiasm to support the war effort.'

↳ **SOURCE G:** *From an article in* The Times, *1918.*

World War Two

The contribution of Empire nations during the next World War, which started just over 20 years after the first, was equally impressive. Look at the map (Source H) carefully, and the other sources, to see the impact of the 'soldiers of empire' during World War Two (1939–1945).

SOURCE H: *The contribution of some of the key colonies of the British Empire during World War Two. It is important to note that many of these nations (like Australia and Canada) were now 'self-governing' and weren't as tied to Britain as they had been years before.* ↘

SOURCE I: *A Canadian recruitment poster.* ↱

"LAND, SEA AND AIR~ WE'RE OVER THERE"

India:
Two and a half million Indians fought with the Brits during World War Two – the largest volunteer army in history! They fought in the Sudan against the Italians, in Libya against the Germans and in Java against the Japanese, amongst others. Over 36,000 Indians were killed and 64,000 were wounded during the war. Indian soldiers, sailors and air crew received over 4000 medals – and 31 Victoria Crosses!

Canada:
Just over a million Canadians fought against Italy and Germany in Europe and Japan in the Pacific region. Canadian troops played a key role in the D-Day landings of 1944 too. Canadian sailors fought bravely to protect ships carrying vital supplies across the Atlantic Ocean. In total, more than 45,000 Canadians lost their lives – and 54,000 were wounded.

The Caribbean:
About 16,000 West Indians volunteered to serve during World War Two. Around 6000 of these served with the Royal Air Force as fighter pilots, bomb aimers and machine gunners. There were 236 West Indian volunteers killed during the war and 265 were wounded.

South Africa:
On the day war broke out (3 September 1939), the South African Prime Minister vowed to keep the country out of the war. But the very next day the South African Parliament voted not to support this stance – and decided to support Britain instead. Over 330,000 South Africans fought for Britain, and over 11,000 were killed.

Africa:
British colonies in West Africa (Gambia, Sierra Leone, the Gold Coast (now Ghana) and Nigeria) served as military bases during the war. Thousands of men and women from British East Africa (Kenya, Uganda and Zanzibar) joined the armed forces, as well as 60,000 from Northern and Southern Rhodesia (now Zambia and Zimbabwe). They generally served as support troops in military hospitals, airfields and naval bases.

Not just about the soldiers

Empire nations did not just contribute to the war effort with soldiers, sailors and air crew. India, for example, served as a training base and provided vast quantities of food to Britain. South Africa supplied vital raw materials such as steel, rubber, platinum and uranium, whilst Canada built thousands of tanks, ships and aircraft. Thousands of West Indian men and women volunteered to fill jobs in Britain where there was a shortage of workers, such as in factories, on farms and in hospitals. Most Empire countries even gave money to Britain to help them fight the war. India, for example, contributed over £170 million to the war effort during World War One – and over £300 million worth of materials and cash in World War Two.

WISE-UP Words

navigator

SOURCE J: *Number 460 Squadron Royal Australian Air Force, with the Lancaster bomber 'G for George' in 1942. They were based in England and the plane carried out 90 bombing missions over Germany.*

Australia:
Almost a million Australians (men and women) served in World War Two. They fought against Germany and Italy in Europe, the Mediterranean and North Africa, as well as against Japan in Southeast Asia. Australia came under direct attack too, as Japanese aircraft bombed towns in northwest Australia and Japanese submarines attacked Sydney Harbour. Over 27,000 Australians lost their lives and over 20,000 were wounded.

New Zealand:
One in ten New Zealanders fought on Britain's side during World War Two – around 160,000 men and women. They were involved in many of the key campaigns in Europe and the Pacific region. A total of 11,928 New Zealanders or 0.73% of the population died. To put this in context, 0.93% of Great Britain's population died, 0.57% of Australia's, 0.40% of Canada's and 0.12% of South Africa's!

SOURCE K: *A poster from World War Two that attempted to show the unity of all the Empire nations.*

'Where Britain goes, we go; where she stands, we stand!'

SOURCE L: *New Zealand's Prime Minister, speaking at the outbreak of war in 1939.*

'The Empire as a whole constituted a far more formidable fighting machine than the UK could ever have been alone.'

SOURCE M: *Historian M.R.D. Foot, commenting on the role of the British Empire during World War Two.*

Work

1 Draw a bar chart showing the number of people who helped Britain during World War Two from at least five colonies. Also include the numbers killed and wounded where possible.

2 Make a list of other ways that countries of the British Empire contributed to the war effort, besides sending soldiers to fight.

3 Give your own opinion – did the Empire help Britain win two World Wars? Write an extended answer, backing up your ideas with evidence.

MISSION ACCOMPLISHED?

• Could you write an extended answer to the following question – 'What was the contribution of the British Empire during World War One and World War Two… and did this contribution help Britain win the wars?'

AFRICA

Until the 1800s, Britain and the other European countries weren't really interested in Africa – unless it was to kidnap people from the west of Africa and take them over to America and the Caribbean to use as slaves! Between 1562 and 1807 (when Britain stopped slave trading), British ships took around three million Africans into slavery. But even as late as 1870, only 10 per cent of Africa was controlled by European countries. Algeria (in the north of Africa) was part of the French Empire; Angola (on the west coast) was controlled by Portugal; and Cape Colony and Natal (now part of South Africa) were controlled by the British. Other than these areas, European countries had no real influence in Africa. Yet by 1900, European nations controlled over 90 per cent of Africa – or 10 million square miles, one-fifth of all the land in the world! Britain itself was one of the nations that took the most land – 16 colonies were added to the British Empire between 1870 and 1900! This Depth Study looks at the story of the British in Africa.

1: The scramble for Africa

MISSION OBJECTIVES

• To explain why Britain joined in the 'scramble for Africa' in the late 1800s.

Between 1880 and 1900, several European nations (including Britain) took over most of the continent of Africa. The race to grab as much of Africa as each nation possibly could became known as the 'scramble for Africa'. So what caused this so-called 'scramble'?

Why Africa?

By the 1860s, France, Germany and the USA had all become powerful nations. They each had huge armies and navies – and their factories produced all sorts of goods that they sold all over the world. Up until then, Britain had been the world's leading power in both industry and trade... but now there were some serious rivals!

Most of the world's richest countries looked to Africa as a way of getting even richer. They thought that if they could take over huge areas of Africa they could sell their goods to the people who lived there – and could also take (or steal) valuable raw materials such as rubber, gold and diamonds from the land itself (see Source A)!

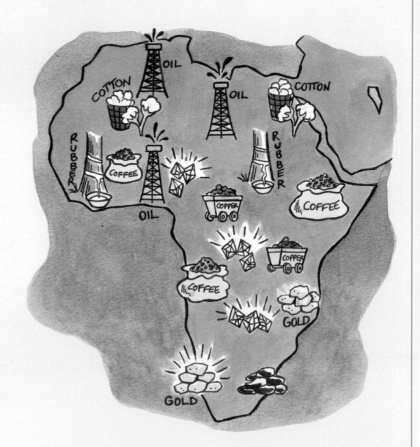

↰ SOURCE A: *Africa's rich supply of raw materials.*

The scramble begins

In the late 1870s several European nations started to 'claim' land in Africa. The French and Belgians began to 'colonize' much of the west of Africa, whilst the Germans and the British were interested in the east and the south. Portugal, Italy and Spain also moved in! To prevent war between the European powers, they even held a conference in Berlin (Germany) during the winter of 1884 to decide which nation could take what! Little attempt was made to understand the wishes or needs of the Africans themselves, so differences in race, language, culture and traditions were ignored as the European nations grabbed what they could (see Source B).

'It's said that our Empire is already big enough and doesn't need extension. That would be true if the world were elastic, but it's not. At present we are "pegging out claims for the future". We have to remember that it's part of our heritage to make sure that the world is shaped by us. It must be English-speaking. We have to look forward to the future of our race. We will fail in our duty if we fail to take our share of the world.'

⌐ SOURCE B: *Lord Rosebery, in a speech made in 1893, during the 'scramble for Africa'. He became Prime Minister a year later.*

![] **FACT** The quickest war in history

In 1896 local leaders in the British colony of Zanzibar (an island off the coast of Africa) chose a ruler that the British government in London didn't approve of. When they refused to change the new ruler, the British government declared war. Nearly 1000 soldiers and sailors (as well as five battleships) began attacking the largest city in Zanzibar at 9.02am on 27 August 1896. At 9.40am the ruler surrendered and a new one was put in his place. The war lasted 38 minutes – the shortest in history!

⌐ SOURCE C: *One of the reasons why European nations took such an interest in Africa in the late 1800s was because of explorers like David Livingstone, pictured here shortly before his death from malaria in 1874. The explorers brought back tales of gold, diamonds and ivory – as well as 'cash crops' such as rubber, coffee and timber. The 'scramble for Africa' was an attempt by Europeans to grab a share of these natural resources!*

The British in Africa

Britain took over 16 huge areas of land (or colonies) in Africa during the 'scramble', including the Sudan, Nigeria, Kenya, Egypt and Northern and Southern Rhodesia (now Zimbabwe and Zambia). In fact, Britain's land ran in an almost unbroken line from Egypt in the north of Africa to South Africa in the south (see Source D). In total, the British had claimed 32 per cent of Africa by 1900 (see Sources E and F)!

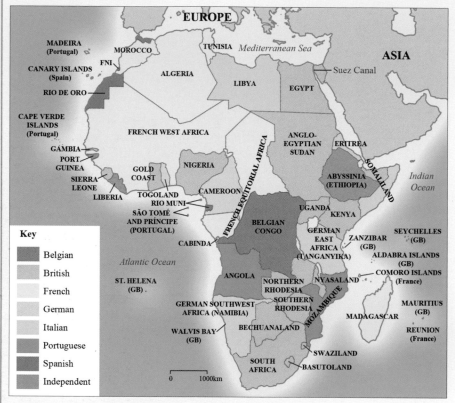

↰ **SOURCE E:** *Africa in 1900, after the 'scramble'.*

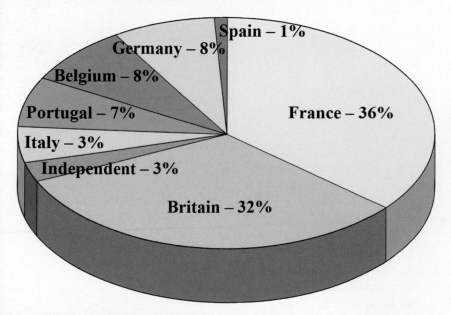

↰ **SOURCE F:** *A pie chart showing the percentage of land colonized by European nations by 1900.*

↰ **SOURCE D:** *A political cartoon from 1892. It features the British politician and businessman Cecil Rhodes, dominating Africa by striding over it. Rhodes, who became the first British ruler of the African colony of Rhodesia (now Zimbabwe), dreamed of a British railway and telegraph system stretching between British colonies in the north and south of Africa.*

African resistance

The African people fought fiercely at times to defend their lands, but the invention of the Maxim gun (a type of machine gun) gave the European armies a major advantage over the Africans, who were mainly armed with handheld spears and swords (see Source H). On occasion African tribes scored major victories over European countries (such as in the Zulu War of 1879), but more often than not the European invaders annihilated the African forces. After they were defeated, many Africans suffered hardship and hunger as their traditional way of life was destroyed. Some were forced to work as cheap labour in mines or on huge British-owned farms growing tea, coffee, cotton or cocoa for export back to Britain.

FACT For medical reasons

One of the reasons that Europeans had not ventured into Africa before the 1870s was that they lacked resistance to diseases they encountered there. After 1870, treatments for combating diseases such as malaria had been invented… meaning that Europeans could explore – and conquer – Africa!

SOURCE G: An African saying.

'When they first came they had the Bible and we had the land. Now we have the Bible and they have the land.'

FACT Suez

One reason that the British were so interested in the African nation of Egypt was the Suez Canal (see Source E). It opened in 1869 and saved ships from having to sail all round Africa to get to India to trade. Britain bought the canal from Egypt in 1875, meaning they now controlled the fastest route to India.

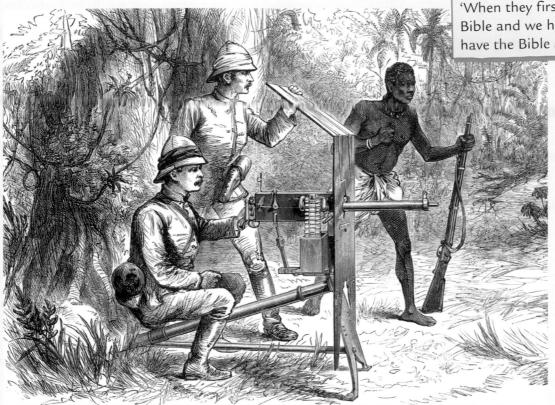

SOURCE H: A Maxim gun in use in Africa in the 1880s. This new gun showed its worth to the British in South Africa in 1893, when 50 Brits fought off 5000 tribal warriors with four Maxims. A famous rhyme of the era went: 'Whatever happens we have got; the Maxim gun and they have not'.

Work

1 a In your own words, explain what is meant by the term 'scramble for Africa'.

  b Why do you think Britain was so keen to take part in the 'scramble'?

2 a Copy this puzzle into your book and fill in the answers to the clues.

  b Now read *down* the puzzle (clue 12) and you will find the name of a famous British explorer. Write a paragraph about him, including how he helped start the 'scramble'.

1. Location of 1884 conference to discuss the 'scramble'.
2. First name of first British ruler of Rhodesia.
3. Profitable trade for Britain between 1562 and 1807.
4. Location of shortest war in history.
5. Britain's main rival in the 'scramble'.
6. New weapon invented in the 1880s.
7. British colonies in Africa: Northern and Southern _____.
8. British colony in North Africa.
9. Very valuable African raw material.
10. Suez _____.
11. 'Bouncy' African raw material.

MISSION ACCOMPLISHED?

• Can you write down at least five facts about 'Britain's African Empire'?

69

Wednesday 22 January 1879 is a remarkable day in the history of the British Empire. On the very same day, two historic battles took place just a few miles apart in southern Africa. At the Battle of Isandlwana, a British force of around 1300 men was wiped out by a Zulu army. Just a short distance away, a group of just 140 British soldiers at a small settlement called Rorke's Drift fought off another Zulu army of 5000 warriors. So who were the Zulus? How did they manage to defeat a modern European army with all the latest weapons? How did the Brits over at Rorke's Drift hold off 5000 warriors? And why were the two sides fighting in the first place?

2: Zulu

MISSION OBJECTIVES

• To understand why Wednesday 22 January 1879 is such a momentous day in British history.

Iklwa – a short, stabbing spear named after the sucking sound it made when it was pulled out of a victim's body!

Assegai – long-bladed spear thrown from a distance.

Knobkerrie – type of club.

Cowhide shield – used to hook the enemy's shield to the side, exposing his ribs for a fatal stab.

Bare feet – Zulus didn't wear shoes but had very tough feet. Warriors could run up to 50 miles a day (nearly two marathons).

Who were the Zulus?

The Zulus were a tribal nation from the southern part of Africa. By the early 1800s there were around 250,000 of them. Under their king, Shaka, they built up a fearsome army of 50,000 warriors, who rampaged through southern Africa destroying other tribes and taking their land (see Source A). Their standard tactic was the famous 'bull horns formation' – see Source B.

By the 1870s a new leader, Cetshwayo, was in charge. The Zulu nation was a threat to the British, who were keen to expand their Empire in this region – especially now that gold and diamonds had been found there. But as far as Cetshwayo was concerned, the British were a threat to his powerful Zulu nation!

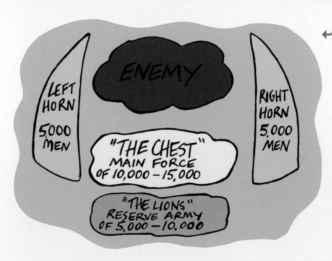

↵ **SOURCE A:** *The 50,000-strong Zulu army was a fierce fighting machine. The men were divided into regiments, or impi, based on age groups, and went through strict training regimes.*

↵ **SOURCE B:** *The Zulu 'bull horns formation'. The main force in the centre would charge at the enemy and fight them hand-to-hand. The quickest warriors would move along the sides of the opposition and try to get around the back. The enemy would then be trapped and encircled. The older, reserve soldiers would sit with their backs to the battle (so they didn't get too excited) until they were needed!*

Conflict

By the 1870s, Zululand (as the Zulu areas were collectively known) had become a large and powerful kingdom. The British wanted the rich Zulu lands for themselves and in December 1878 they gave the Zulu king an **ultimatum**. He had to get rid of the Zulu army, allow British settlers to move into the area and only make decisions after consulting the British… or face invasion! The Zulu king gave no reply – so in January 1879 a British army invaded Zululand. The first fighting between Zulus and Brits took place on Wednesday 22 January 1879. It was a legendary day!

Read the following remarkable true story carefully.

WISE-UP Words

ultimatum

1 The British Army of 6000 soldiers first marched into Zululand on 11 January 1879.

The Brits were helped by around 8000 local African troops (not Zulus – obviously!).

2 The plan was to split the Army into three and march towards the royal capital of Zululand – Ulundi.

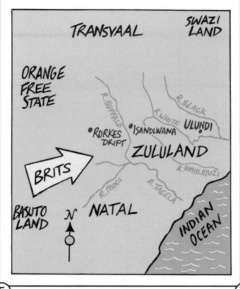

3 The Brits left a small group of around 140 soldiers at a former trading post, 'Rorke's Drift'.

A few hundred Africans stayed there too, to help the Brits. Rorke's Drift was to act as a supply depot and medical treatment centre.

4 By 20 January the main army got to a hill ten miles from Rorke's Drift, called Isandlwana, and made camp there.

At 4:00am on 22 January, Lord Chelmsford (leader of the army) took two-thirds of the soldiers off to find the Zulu army.

5 The other third stayed behind. Little did they know that 20,000 Zulu warriors were on the other side of the hill!

At 11:00am, sentries spotted Zulu warriors on the hill. And from over three miles away, thousands of Zulu warriors began to charge!

6 The Zulus and the soldiers at the camp fought hand-to-hand for over four hours.

A message from Isandlwana got to Lord Chelmsford – but he thought it was a false alarm and didn't return to camp!

7 The Zulu army massacred the Brits and their African helpers. Of 1700 Brits and Africans, 1350 died.

Only a few hundred survived, managing to escape into the African countryside.

8 At around 4:00pm, some survivors managed to get back to Rorke's Drift with news of the attack.

IT WAS A MASSACRE

HELP ME

The men at Rorke's Drift were warned that the victorious Zulus could be on their way!

9 The men at Rorke's Drift decided to stay and defend it, although some of the African helpers ran away!

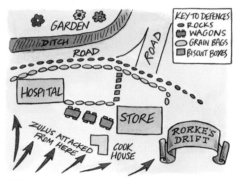

They used rocks, wagons, grain bags and even biscuit boxes to build up defences! Only around 120 men could fight. Some had to stay in the hospital!

10 The Zulu attack finally came at around 5:00pm. Some of the Zulus were now armed with guns too!

There were 4000 to 5000 Zulus in the attack, mainly the reserve warriors who didn't fight at Isandlwana. They used their classic 'bull horns formation'.

11 Within two hours the hospital was on fire and had to be evacuated. A soldier with a broken leg was pulled out... but broke his other leg in the process!

PRIVATE HOOK

PRIVATE CONLEY

By 7:00pm the Brits had retreated to the area around the storeroom. Miraculously, by 10:00pm only 15 of them had been killed and eight seriously wounded.

12 At around 4:00am the attacks stopped, and at 8:00am Lord Chelmsford's army finally arrived.

AT LAST!

WE'RE SAVED!

In total, 370 Zulu dead were counted!

13 Eleven Victoria Crosses (VCs) were later awarded to the soldiers of Rorke's Drift. Five more got Distinguished Conduct Medals.

THE VC IS BRITAIN'S HIGHEST BRAVERY AWARD

MORE VCs WERE AWARDED FOR THE BATTLE OF RORKE'S DRIFT THAN FOR ANY OTHER BATTLE IN BRITISH MILITARY HISTORY

14 The defeat at Isandlwana shocked Britain! Not surprisingly, the newspapers focused on the heroic defence of Rorke's Drift instead.

To many it was unthinkable that 'native warriors' armed with spears could challenge the might of the British Army... but they had!

The aftermath

Wednesday 22 January 1879 is a legendary day in British history – for two opposing reasons. It was the day when the British Army performed one of their most heroic feats (at Rorke's Drift) – yet also suffered one of their most humiliating defeats (at Isandlwana). When news got back to Britain of the events of 22 January the response was pride, shock… and uproar! It has even been argued that the awarding of eleven Victoria Crosses for the bravery shown by the men of Rorke's Drift was done to take the British public's minds off the defeat at Isandlwana. As the historian Dr Saul David put it in 2009: 'Though undeniably heroic, the importance of the defence of Rorke's Drift has been exaggerated by both the generals and politicians of the period, to diminish the impact of Isandlwana'.

The end of the Zulu War

The Zulu War continued for another six months after the events of 22 January. In March a Zulu army attacked another British Army camp – but the Zulus were defeated. Finally, the Brits organized a massive attack on the royal city of Ulundi in July 1879 and the Zulus were defeated once and for all. Their king, Cetshwayo, was captured and sent to London. He returned to southern Africa in 1883, but died shortly afterwards. By then, Zululand had been split up into 13 different regions… and was firmly under the control of the British! Yet another part of the world had been absorbed into the British Empire.

Work

1 a Who were the Zulus?
  b Describe how the Zulus fought. Use a diagram to help you if you wish.

2 a Imagine you are a British journalist in South Africa in 1879. Write an article for a British newspaper explaining what happened on 22 January.
  b How would you expect the British public to react to your article?
  c How might an account of the battles from the point of view of the Zulus be different?

3 Look at Source C. Suppose you had seen this painting at an exhibition in 1880. Describe your reaction to it and then write a short story or poem based on it.

↰ **SOURCE C:** *A painting by A.A. de Neu called 'The Defence of Rorke's Drift' (1880). The painter visited the location of the battle shortly after it happened. Note the dog in the painting. The dog (called Pip) belonged to one of the soldiers and played his part in the defence by running along the barricades barking as the enemy approached. Pip survived but his owner didn't. However, Pip was adopted by another soldier and brought back to Britain. Pip is buried with his owner in Kensal Green Cemetery in London!*

MISSION ACCOMPLISHED?

• Can you think of reasons why Wednesday 22 January 1879 could be viewed in both positive and negative ways by British people at the time… and today?

Between 1899 and 1902 the British fought a war in southern Africa called the Boer War. As a result, the British Army needed lots of men to fight. However, around 40 per cent of the men who volunteered were too unhealthy to be soldiers. In some big cities an amazing 90 per cent of men weren't fit enough! This not only worried army leaders – it worried the British government too! Within five years of the end of the Boer War, the government had introduced reforms aimed at getting Britain fitter… including free school meals for Britain's poorest kids! So what was the Boer War all about? Why were so many fit young men needed to fight in it? And how, exactly, did the Boer War lead to free school meals?

3: How did a war in Africa change British schools?

—————————————— MISSION OBJECTIVES ——————————————
• To understand how an 'Empire war' led to fundamental changes in the way Britain cared for its most vulnerable citizens.

Who were the Boers?

In the 1800s two groups of Europeans competed for control of southern Africa – the Brits and the Boers. The Boers were descendants of Dutch settlers who had gone to southern Africa in the 1600s. Their colony was called 'Cape Colony' – but the Brits took it over in 1815. The Boers then went north and set up two new colonies called the Transvaal and the Orange Free State.

In 1867 diamonds were discovered in the new Boer states – and then gold in the 1880s! Soon, thousands of Brits flooded in and opened dozens of mines. The Boers felt threatened and the Boer leaders taxed the British miners heavily. During the 1890s relations between the Brits and Boers got worse – and in 1899 war broke out (see Source A)!

⤦ SOURCE A: *Boers and Brits do battle during the Boer war.*

SOURCE B: *Inside a concentration camp. Sadly, a British invention.* ⤳

The Boer War

Early on, the small Boer army of 50,000 stunned the Brits with a series of victories. The British responded by sending half a million soldiers to fight them. The British Army used all the hi-tech weaponry they had – machine guns, modern rifles and high explosive shells. Yet the Boers refused to surrender and carried out dozens of small raids on British camps, railways and mines. So the Brits responded savagely.

'Scorched earth'

The British commander during the Boer war, General Kitchener, decided that the only way to get the Boers to surrender was to introduce a 'scorched earth' policy.

British soldiers were instructed to burn down Boer farms, kill the animals, destroy crops and poison drinking wells. Then Boer men, women and children and their black servants were rounded up into 'concentration camps'. Out of 116,000 Boers put in these camps, 28,000 (mainly children) died due to the poor conditions (see Source B).

Peace at last

By 1902 both sides were exhausted so peace talks began. It was agreed that the Boer states would become British colonies, but the Boers were promised that they could make many of the key decisions in running their lands. In 1910 the Boer states joined with Cape Colony and Natal (the other British colonies in the area) to form the 'Union of South Africa' – still part of the British Empire, but a **dominion** that ran its own affairs!

Boer War controversy

The Boer War was Britain's biggest 'Empire war'. Nearly 500,000 Brits had fought in it – and 8000 had died in battle. Another 13,000 died from illnesses! The Boers lost 4000 soldiers and over 28,000 civilians. The war showed how determined the British were to hold onto their Empire – but some British people began to lose their enthusiasm for the Empire when they realized how brutal the British had been!

Problems back home

The Boer War had an unexpected consequence! Young British men had volunteered to fight in their thousands, but over a third of them were classed as 'unfit for duty'. This worried the government. Unless something was done, how was Britain going to fight its wars in the future?

Around the same time, several special investigations into the lives of the poor started to make headlines. One report found that around 30 per cent of Londoners were so poor that they didn't have enough money to eat properly – despite having full-time jobs!

Finally, in 1906, the government decided to act. One of the first moves was to introduce free school meals for the poorest children (see Source C). Other measures included free medical checks and treatment in schools (see Source D).

After helping children, the government moved onto other sections of society. They introduced unemployment benefit ('the dole'), sickness pay and old age pensions. They even built Britain's first job centres. Indeed, it seems that a distant African war led to many of the ideas that still help the most vulnerable people in our society today.

↵ **SOURCE D:** *An anxious mother watches the doctor examine her son in one of Britain's first free medical checks.*

WISE-UP Words

dominion

! FACT The Kop

One of the most famous battles of the Boer War was fought at a place called Spion Kop in January 1900. Many football clubs, including Liverpool, Sheffield United, Leicester City, Preston North End and Birmingham City named stands in their football grounds after this battle.

SOURCE C: *A typical week of free school meals. By 1914, over 158,000 children were having free meals once a day.* ⤵

THIS WEEK'S MENU

Monday: Tomato soup – Currant roly-poly pudding
Tuesday: Meat pudding – Rice pudding
Wednesday: Yorkshire pudding, gravy, peas – Rice pudding and sultanas
Thursday: Vegetable soup – Currant pastry or fruit tart
Friday: Stewed fish, parsley sauce, peas, mashed potatoes – Blancmange

Work

1 Explain the following terms:
   • Boer • 'scorched earth'
   • concentration camp
   • Union of South Africa.

2 Look at Sources A and D. In your own words, explain how the war shown in Source A led to the medical examination happening in Source D.

3 Look at Source C. Choose one meal and write a few sentences comparing it to what you had for dinner on the same day. Which was healthier?

—— MISSION ACCOMPLISHED? ——

• Can you explain, in no more than 50 words, how the Boer War changed British society?

Between 1880 and 1900 nearly 90 per cent of Africa was divided up amongst the European powers. By 1900 Britain controlled 16 African colonies, including Nigeria, the Sudan, Kenya, Egypt, Northern and Southern Rhodesia (now Zimbabwe and Zambia) and South Africa (see Source A). However, just over 100 years later, *none* of these colonies are part of the British Empire any more – in fact, they are all fully-functioning independent states. So how, why and when did independence in Africa happen?

4: Independence in Africa

MISSION OBJECTIVES

• To understand the impact of World War Two on the African independence movement.

The beginning of the end of the Empire

By the time World War One started in 1914, several of Britain's colonies – such as Canada, Australia and New Zealand – had been running their own affairs for years. In Africa, South Africa had been self-governing since 1910 and in 1922 Egypt became independent too. Some argued that Britain was happier to allow white self-rule than it was to allow black or Asian self-rule – and indeed, the colonies that gained independence first all contained a majority of white settlers. But World War Two changed things forever!

The impact of World War Two

World War Two cost the lives of millions of soldiers and civilians in most areas of the world. Just as in World War One, soldiers in the colonies joined the army of the British Empire to fight. In Africa, soldiers from all the British colonies fought against Nazi Germany, Italy and Japan. The colonies themselves served as military bases and supplied food and other materials to the British.

By the end of World War Two, many of Britain's colonies were demanding the right to rule themselves. The war had cost billions of pounds and thousands of Brits had died – so Britain no longer had the military strength or the wealth to hold onto its colonies. Also, the Africans who had fought for Britain had felt they were fighting to defend freedom – and were getting increasingly frustrated that their own countries were not yet free!

The Gold Coast leads the way

When India won its independence from Britain in 1947 it led to a whole host of other countries demanding their freedom. In 1957 the Gold Coast (as it was known under British rule) got its independence and became Ghana. Nigeria (1960), Sierra Leone (1961), Uganda (1962) and Kenya (1963) followed soon after.

Independence for these nations was achieved fairly peacefully. There were riots in some places like Kenya, but on the whole the transfer of power went smoothly. Newly independent nations like Nigeria, Gambia and Kenya were invited to join the **British Commonwealth**, an organization of independent, free countries with close cultural, trade and sporting links to Britain.

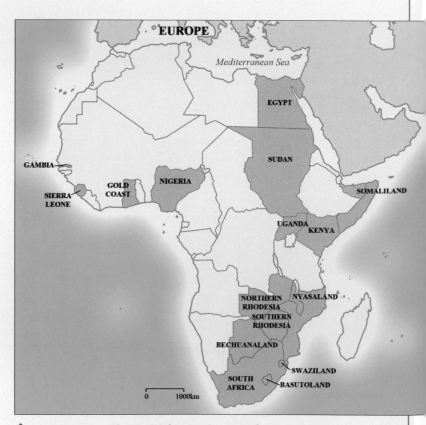

⤓ SOURCE A: *The British Empire in Africa in 1900.*

SOURCE B: Celebrating independence in Kenya in 1963.

WISE-UP Words

apartheid
British Commonwealth

↳ SOURCE C: *The Commonwealth Games is a sports competition held every four years in one of the former colonies of the British Empire. Athletes from former colonies are invited to participate.*

A new Africa

For many newly independent nations, freedom brought difficulties as well as benefits. Some nations, like Egypt, have developed thriving tourist industries, while others have made good use of raw materials such as rubber, gold and diamonds. However, some countries have seen rivalries between tribes flare up into bloody civil war. This happened in Nigeria in the 1960s, Uganda in the 1980s, and Sierra Leone in the 1990s. Many new nations have struggled to create their own systems of government, build up their own industry and trade, and cope with internal divisions. Perhaps the greatest problem the newly independent nations have had to deal with is poverty. Of the 25 poorest countries in the world, 17 are in Africa… and despite loans and aid from richer countries, the problems of poverty and long-term debt remain.

SOURCE D: *In recent years there have been several high profile campaigns and events, such as Make Poverty History and Live 8, aimed at helping some of the world's poorest countries, including many in Africa. Comic Relief, for example, raises millions with its Red Nose Day to fund aid projects all over Africa.* ↗

! FACT South Africa

South Africa has been running itself since 1910. After World War Two they introduced what was known as **apartheid**. This means that the white government introduced racist laws to keep whites and blacks separate (or segregated). For example, education and medical care were segregated, and blacks had worse services than whites. Countries around the world criticized South Africa, and refused to trade or play sport with them. Apartheid eventually ended in 1994 and Nelson Mandela (who was imprisoned for 27 years under the old regime) became South Africa's first democratically-elected President.

Work

1 In your own words, explain how World War Two helped lead to the independence of many British colonies in Africa.

2 Name the African country that became independent from Britain in each of the following years.
▪ 1910 ▪ 1922 ▪ 1957 ▪ 1963.

3 a Explain what challenges many African nations have faced since independence.
  b Have you ever 'helped out' an African nation? Think carefully – there are lots of ways that you might have done.

___ **MISSION ACCOMPLISHED?** ___

• Can you identify at least two ways that World War Two contributed to Britain's gradual withdrawal from Africa?

What is the legacy of the British Empire?

MISSION OBJECTIVES

- To be able to identify three ways in which we still remember the British Empire in Britain today... and three ways in which the British Empire is still remembered around the world.

Before starting this topic, you need to understand what is meant by the term 'legacy'. Why not discuss what you think this word means with someone sitting near you, or discuss it as a class? For those of you without enough time to discuss what 'legacy' means, a definition has been provided for you in Source A. So what has the British Empire left behind that is remembered? In what ways does it impact on our lives today? Indeed, what is the legacy of the British Empire?

As you might expect, the legacy of the British Empire is huge. After all, at one point the Empire covered a quarter of the world and contained over 400 million people in over 50 colonies, and it lasted for hundreds of years. But not only is there a legacy of the British Empire all over the world – there is a legacy in Britain today. The following sections – 'Legacy of Empire in Britain' and 'Legacy of Empire across the world' – examine what aspects of the Empire still have an impact on our lives today.

'Legacy is what someone or something is remembered for or what they leave behind that is remembered. It is usually someone or something that made an impact at the time – and still makes an impact today.'

↳ **SOURCE A:** *An excellent definition of the word 'legacy' – as written collectively by a Year 9 class after a brainstorm session at Castle High School, Dudley in December 2009.*

The legacy of Empire in Britain

Just after World War Two, the British Parliament introduced a new law – the British Nationality Act. Britain was really short of workers at this time, and the new law meant that all people of the Empire (now called the Commonwealth by many) – were given British passports and were allowed to live and work in Britain. Most of these people had been brought up speaking English and educated to believe in the importance of Britain. And within 20 years, thousands of people from all over the Empire had come to settle in 'the motherland'.

Although many people in Britain were alarmed by the arrival of newcomers from different religions, cultures and races, it didn't stop these people building new lives and making their homes in Britain. At first the immigrants were often treated like strange outsiders, but gradually, over the years, they have made a massive contribution to British society and culture. Look carefully through Sources B to H, which examine the impact of Empire on our lives today.

Country of origin	Words now used in everyday English
India	pyjamas, bungalow, cot, bangle, loot, mugger, pundit, shampoo, sentry, cash, mouse
Africa	banjo, cola, coffee, jazz, zombie, trek, safari, banana, jukebox
Australia	boomerang, kangaroo
Native America	chocolate, shack, anorak, barbeque, jaguar, canoe, hurricane, chilli, potato

↳ **SOURCE B:** *Examples of words from all parts of the British Empire that have gradually made their way into the English language.*

SOURCE C: *The Great British meal? The food brought to Britain from the Empire has revolutionized our eating habits. The curry now rivals the Sunday roast and fish and chips as Britain's national dish. Chicken Tikka Masala is the country's best-selling 'ready meal' and 'going for a curry' has become a weekly event for millions of Brits. It is now such a part of life in Britain that a song called* Vindaloo *(a hot spicy curry) became an anthem for the English football team!* ↱

⬑ SOURCE D: *The legacy of Britain's Empire is still alive in some of its finest buildings. African, Indian and far Eastern designs were copied by designers in Britain. The Royal Pavilion in Brighton clearly shows the Indian influence on its design.*

SOURCE E:
Immigration from the Empire has had a big influence on British music. Panjabi MC, for example, is a British Indian musician from Coventry whose music mixes bhangra and hip-hop. His single 'Mundian To Bach Ke' used the theme from Knight Rider mixed with bhangra and has been sampled by Jay-Z. His remix of 'Chaiyya Chaiyya' was used on the soundtrack for the film Inside Man, *starring Denzel Washington.*

⬎ SOURCE G. *Another legacy of the British Empire is a special award known as an 'Order of the British Empire' (OBE). They are given out to people who the Queen believes have made a significant contribution to the nation. All sorts of people can receive them – from soldiers to teachers to pop stars! Here, author JK Rowling is holding her OBE, awarded for 'services to children's literature' in 2001.*

⬑ SOURCE F: *Britain's sports teams have benefitted from the influence of Empire for years. Recently, for example, England's cricket team has been captained by Nasser Hussain (who was born in India) and Kevin Pietersen (born and raised in South Africa).*

SOURCE H: ↱
One of the most significant legacies of Empire is 'multicultural Britain'.
The diverse nature of the population is reflected here, with Queen Elizabeth II meeting with both the Pearly King and Queen (an East End of London tradition) and the Newham Mayor, Sukhdev Singh Marway. In modern Britain there is rarely a workplace, sports team or classroom without someone whose ancestors were once part of the British Empire.

Work

1 In your own words, explain what is meant by the word 'legacy'.

2 a What was the British Nationality Act?
b This Act caused a lot of controversy at the time. Why do you think many people in Britain objected to it?

3 Make a list of at least five ways in which the British Empire has had an impact on life in Britain today.

Legacy of Empire across the world

Even though the British Empire no longer exists, its legacy survives in different parts of the world today.

The Commonwealth

Nearly all former Empire colonies now belong to an organization called 'The Commonwealth of Nations'. It promotes democracy, human rights, good government, fair laws and world peace. There are currently 54 member countries, containing 1.7 billion people (30% of the world's population) and covering a quarter of the world's land surface!

Sport

Organized ball games – like football, rugby and cricket – became very popular in Britain in the 1800s. When Brits went out to live in the colonies, they took their love of these sports with them. As a result, some of them became very popular in Empire countries. Snooker, for example, was invented by British Army officers stationed in India, and the top ten cricketing nations today are all former colonies of the British Empire.

↵ **SOURCE I:** *'The Commonwealth' holds its own sport event every four years. This is a photograph from the 2006 Commonwealth Games, held in Melbourne, Australia. It shows athletes from the former colonies of Mauritius, Jamaica, New Zealand, Nigeria and Australia (as well as England's Marlon Devonish – top).*

A · GLORIOUS · COMPANY · THE · FLOWER · OF · MEN

TO · SERVE · AS · MODEL · FOR · THE · MIGHTY · WORLD

BRITISH · EMPIRE EXHIBITION · 1924
APRIL TO OCTOBER —— WEMBLEY · LONDON

The English language

When a nation became part of the British Empire, the Brits made sure that English became the language used there in all trading, industry and business. As a result, English became (and remains) an official language in dozens of former Empire countries, including the USA, Australia, New Zealand, Jamaica, Nigeria, Kenya, South Africa, Canada and India. The map shows all the places where it is an official language. Over one billion people worldwide speak English today.

Democracy

Britain has always been very proud of its system of democracy – that is, that ordinary citizens can vote for politicians who run Britain on their behalf. In other words, 'people power'. In many of Britain's former colonies this system of democracy was copied. Australia, Canada, India and New Zealand, for example, all have elected politicians who work at a Parliament. Indeed, India is the largest democratic country in the world!

Driving on the left and English law

In Britain we drive on the left-hand side of the road – and so do most of Britain's former colonies, such as Australia, Kenya, Jamaica, South Africa, India and Pakistan. This 'road rule' was not the only law that stayed in the colonies once they became independent from Britain. Many colonies kept the idea of 'English Common Law' when setting up their legal systems.

Common Law is the idea that people on trial are 'innocent until proven guilty' and have the right to a fair trial that is tried in the same way as other trials in the past. Common Law systems are used in many former colonies of the British Empire, including the USA, Pakistan, India, Ghana, Canada, South Africa and New Zealand.

The Imperial System

For centuries the British have used a system of measuring and weighing called the 'Imperial System'. This system was also introduced across the British Empire… and is still used in many former Empire countries today. For example, we still measure height in feet and inches, distance in miles, speed in miles per hour, weight in stones and pounds and milk and beer in pints. All these are Imperial weights and measures.

Work

Either:

Design a poster that celebrates the British Empire and its contribution to the world. You can use as many pictures and diagrams as you wish – but only 50 words!

Or:

Imagine you have been asked to put on an exhibition called 'The Legacy of the British Empire'. You must use just ten exhibits to demonstrate the impact the Empire had on Britain and the world. What exhibits will you choose? You will need to use your imagination and think how you can demonstrate the power, influence and legacy of the Empire using only ten different pictures, artefacts or items. Make sure you write a detailed label to go with each of your choices!

! FACT The Empire Exhibition 1924

A huge exhibition to celebrate the achievements of the British Empire was held in London in 1924. The poster on the opposite page was one of many that advertised it. A new stadium, called the 'Empire Stadium', was built to host the exhibition. When it finished, the stadium was used for the annual FA Cup Final. By the 1930s it had become known as 'Wembley' after the area of London were it was located.

✚ Hungry for MORE

Another legacy of the British Empire is the hundreds of places around the world named after great British soldiers, explorers, kings and queens. New Zealand's capital city (Wellington), the Cook Islands (Captain Cook) and Africa's largest lake (Victoria) are three good examples. But can you find ten further examples of towns, cities, regions, states, areas, countries, lakes or mountains in the former British Empire that are named after famous Brits?

—MISSION ACCOMPLISHED?—

• Can you give three examples of the British Empire's legacy in Britain and abroad?

Was the British Empire a good or a bad thing?

────────── **MISSION OBJECTIVES** ──────────

- To form your own opinion – was the British Empire a force for good or not... or does the answer lie somewhere in the middle?

Over the last hundred years the British Empire has gradually got smaller and smaller, as more and more countries have begun to rule themselves. By 1910 its four big settler colonies – Canada, Australia, New Zealand and South Africa – had all become self-governing, and in 1931 they achieved full independence. India followed in 1947, when Britain was weakened by World War Two, and then gradually nearly all the colonies in Africa and the rest of the world became independent too. Believe it or not, the British Empire does still exist – there are 14 colonies that never left the Empire, mainly small islands dotted around the world. Today they are called 'British Overseas Territories' (see Source A).

It might not look like much today, but in its time the British Empire had a huge influence on the rest of the world. But was it a force for good, or were its impacts mainly negative? The following are all examples of opinions about the British Empire. Some are positive about it, whilst others are negative. Some are both! Read through them carefully – your task at the end will be to organize the statements… and then form an opinion of your own.

The British Empire had land in every continent, and contained some of the world's highest mountains, biggest lakes, longest rivers and most famous landmarks. The countries it ruled are now some of the richest and most powerful in the world – like the USA, Australia and South Africa. What an achievement!

The British Empire brought good things to places like India and Africa (railways, hospitals, law and order and so on) but at a cost. The cost was the people's right to govern themselves.

The British Empire was about three things – God, gold and glory! It's a myth that it was about helping countries. All the empire builders cared about was converting natives to Christianity, personal glory and making money.

The British thought they were racially superior to the people they conquered. We say it's wrong for the racist Nazis to try and take over Europe in World War Two, so why isn't it wrong for racist Brits to try and take over the rest of the world?

The British did some awful things – their role in the slave trade, the Amritsar Massacre in India and the use of concentration camps in the Boer War, for example.

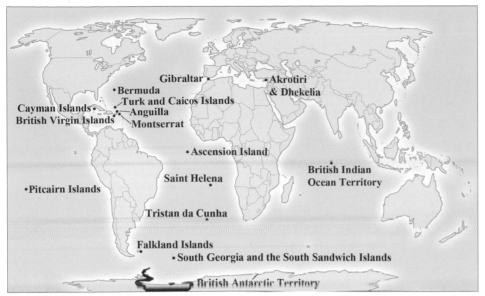

↳ **SOURCE A:** *The British Empire today – or the 'British Overseas Territory', as it is correctly known.*

Britain was always at war in one part of the Empire or another. The people in the colonies rebelled against the British because the British just weren't wanted!

The Brits brought law and order, transport, education, banking and medicine to places all over the world. They left great universities, team sports, the English language and the idea of democracy. Of course the British Empire was a force for good!

When they pulled out of India, the British left chaos behind. The divisions between India and Pakistan, and those in many former colonies in Africa too, can be traced back to the British Empire.

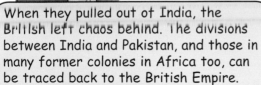

The British Empire was better than other empires at the time. The French tried to make Africans into Frenchmen... or else! And Belgium and Portugal ran their colonies very harshly. Britain thought of itself more as a mother country helping the colonies to develop.

Work

1 Make two lists, one of all the bad things about the British Empire and one of all the good things. Don't just use the opinions on this page to help you – use your own knowledge gained from all your studies of the British Empire.

2 The British Empire has always been the subject of fierce debate. There have even been calls to ban the teaching of the British Empire in schools! Imagine your headteacher has *banned* the teaching of the British Empire at your school. Write them a letter explaining whether you support their decision or not.

- A **basic** letter will say whether you agree with the decision or not and list some good and/or bad points about the Empire.

- A **better** letter will say whether we should study the British Empire or not – and give one or two reasons why. It will also include some basic facts about the Empire.

- A **very good** letter will give several reasons why we should or should not study the British Empire – and back up these opinions with facts and figures.

- The **best** letters will do all of the above – but will cover both sides of the argument and explain why we should study both bad and good things in history lessons.

MISSION ACCOMPLISHED?

- Do you know what the British Empire consists of today?

- Do you understand why people disagree over the importance, impact and legacy of the British Empire?

Have you been learning? 2

TASK 1 Empire anagrams

In the anagram list you will find:

a The Queen of England who had two Australian colonies named after her in the 1850s.

b The British politician and businessman who became the first British ruler of the African colony of Rhodesia.

c The World War One soldier from what is now Pakistan who was awarded a VC in 1914.

d The Maori Chief who took on the British in the Flagpole War in 1845.

e A Viceroy of India who restored the Taj Mahal.

f The British Commander who introduced the 'scorched earth' policy during the Boer War.

g The Aboriginal freedom fighter who avoided capture for 12 years and once survived being shot seven times.

h A famous English explorer in Africa who died from malaria in 1874.

i The first Brit to land in Australia.

j The first Englishman to sail around the world.

All the answers are given below, but in the wrong order and with their letters mixed up. Can you unravel them?

DUDHADAK HANK	CLICE DOESHR
DROL NOCRUZ	IRS FISCRAN RAKED
NITAPAC SAMEJ OOKC	LEGRENA RENTHIECK
AVIOCTIR	VADDI ENTIVLINGSO
ENOH KEEH	UWEMPLYU

TASK 2 Odd two out

Here are eight sentences about the British Empire. Each sentence has two errors. One is a spelling mistake and the other is a factual error. When you have spotted the mistakes, write each sentence out correctly.

a The first few attempts by English settlers to set up colonys in North America were failures. However, all that changed in 1607 when a new colony called Elizabethtown became a success.

b The colonies in North America were an important part of the British Empire for many years. The settlers grew tobacco, coton and many other crops that they sold back in Britain and Europe. But eventually the settlers in America decided to break free from British rule and in 1876 they declared their independence.

c The American War of Independance lasted for several years. Thousands of troops from Britain went over to fight the rebel settlers. Finally though, the settlers won and the 14 British colonies in America became independent.

d In the 1700s British merchants began trading with India. They set up trading posts on the Indian coast and gradually, over the next century, took more and more Indian land. In 1757 many Indian soldiers rebelled against British control of there land but the rebellion was crushed brutally.

e India was one of the largest and richest of all the countries in Britain's Empire. In fact, Queen Victoria was so proud of it that she used to call herself 'Top Dog of India'. Many ordinary people treasured the colony too and called it 'the Jewel in the Crown' of Briton's Empire.

f In April 1770 Captain John Cook landed on the east coast of Australia at Botany Bay and claimed it for Britain. Over the next few years, thousands of settlers went over to Austrailia to live. Britain even used it as a place to send criminals.

g In the 1880s several Europeon nations took over large areas of land in Africa. This is often known as the 'scramble for Africa'. Britain took control of 16 colonies in Africa including Egypt, Nigeria, Kenya, South Africa and Algeria.

h The British Empire began to break up after World War Two. Ghana won its independence in 1947 and many African colonies then followed. However, most of the former colonies are still linked to Britain through an organization called 'the Commonwealth of Nations'. It promotes democracy, human rights, good goverment and world peace.

TASK 3 Sort the stories

There are always at least two ways of looking at any event in history. Here are 12 headlines that *could* have appeared in newspapers during the era of the British Empire. They are about six different events.

a Pair up the headlines so that you have one in favour of (or for) each event and one not in favour of (or against) the event.

b Write down a short description of the six events to which the headlines refer.

c For each event write an alternative headline that is not biased.

d Choose one of the events and write a news story about it that is not biased.

Zulus bravely defend their homeland

We're off to spank the Yanks

British soldiers attacked by Indian traitors

Courageous settlers seek new life down under

Africa exploited by greedy Brits

America should be for Americans

Heroic Brits fight off Zulu savages

Britain invades yet another continent

Why compensation after all these years?

Brave Indians stand up to foreign oppressors

Britain set to civilize Africa

Time to make up and pay up for Britain's role in slave trade

TASK 4 Elements of an empire

The British Empire was made up of two main parts – the ruling or 'mother' country (Britain) and the areas that it ruled (the colonies). Some elements of what made up the British Empire as a whole were supplied by Britain, and others were provided by the colonies.

a In pairs (or on your own if you wish!) draw up a table putting each of the elements in the list below under one of these two headings – 'mother country' or 'colonies'.

b Now use your two lists to help you answer this question:

What is the relationship between the 'mother country' and its colonies?

A: Lots of raw materials like cotton, iron ore, timber or diamonds.

B: A strong, well-equipped army.

C: Lots of people to provide cheap labour.

D: A strong navy to protect trade ships.

E: Weak government.

F: A huge population to sell goods to.

G: Advanced technology and high-tech equipment to mine, farm and transport raw materials.

H: A well-educated, established group of managers and clerks to organize and run things.

I: A large fleet of transport ships to transport cargo.

J: Many factories to manufacture goods made from raw materials.

K: Rich businessmen and entrepreneurs to invest in new ideas and production methods.

L: A population made up mainly of farmers (or hunter-gatherers) rather than factory workers.

85

Glossary

Abolition Doing away with something; for example getting rid of slavery.

Aboriginal Australians The native people who lived in Australia before Captain Cook and other Europeans arrived.

Apartheid A policy of racist separation; laws to keep white and black people segregated (apart).

Assassinated Murdered for political reasons.

Botanists Scientists specializing in the study of plants.

British Commonwealth An organization of nations consisting of Britain and some of its former colonies; now independent, free countries, but retaining close cultural, trade and sporting links to Britain.

Cartridge Cylindrical case used to contain bullets and gunpowder.

Ceasefire A temporary stop to war, in which each side agrees to suspend attacks.

Colony/colonies Areas or countries controlled by another country; for example, Britain controlled a huge number of colonies, which made up its Empire.

Compensation Money or other benefits given to make up for injury or other damage caused.

Democracy A form of government where the people of the country elect the leaders.

Dependencies Another word for colonies.

Disputes Arguments; disagreements.

Dominant Having influence and control.

Dominion/dominions Another word for colony/colonies.

East India Company An English company formed in 1600 to trade with India.

Empires Collections of different areas or countries controlled by one 'mother' country; for example, Britain had the largest empire in the world by 1900.

Hunter-gatherers People who survive by gathering edible plants and killing wild animals to eat.

Immigrants People who leave the country where they were born to live in another country, where they settle permanently.

Imperial System A system of measuring and weighing, used for centuries in Britain and still used in many former Empire countries (examples of imperial weights and measures are pounds, inches and pints).

Independence Freedom from control or influence of another.

Lashed Beaten with a whip or rope as a form of punishment.

Legacy What someone or something is remembered for or what they leave behind that is remembered. It is usually someone or something that made an impact at the time – and still makes an impact today.

Maoris Tribespeople who settled in New Zealand about 1000 years ago.

Maroons Runaway slaves who lived in the West Indies (mainly in Jamaica).

Maxim gun A machine gun.

Missionaries Religious people sent to convert natives of another country to a religion (for example, Christianity).

Moscow Company An English company formed to trade with Russia.

Mughals Muslims who ruled India in the 1500s.

Mutiny Open rebellion against authority.

Muzzle A device strapped over the mouth.

Navigator A person who plots the course for an aircraft or a ship.

Nomadic Having no fixed home; travelling to different places to hunt and gather food.

Partition Dividing something into parts.

Plantations Large farms on which crops are grown.

Privateers Officers of privately owned ships, authorized by a country's leaders to attack ships from enemy countries.

Protectorates Another word for colonies.

Puritans A type of English Protestant; strict Christians.

Racism Believing that a particular race is superior to other races.

Rebels People who forcibly oppose authority.

Renaissance A cultural 'rebirth'; used to describe the period in the late 1400s when people such as writers, mathematicians and scientists learnt new things and experimented with new ideas.

Revolution The overthrow of a government by the people who are ruled.

Self-government Government of a country or area by its own people.

Sepoy A native Indian soldier.

Slave triangle The trading of slaves between Africa, the Americas and Europe.

Spice Islands A group of islands in eastern Indonesia now known as the Moluccas, originally settled by the Portuguese but later taken by the Dutch.

'Stolen Generations' Aboriginal Australian children taken from their families in the 1800s to go and live in white Christian homes.

Trading stations Large warehouses at ports where goods were stored and where trading took place.

Transportation Being moved from one place to another; for example, the transportation of British convicts to Australia.

'Trash gangs' Slave children who were made to weed British plantations.

Ultimatum A final demand.

Viceroy Someone who rules a country, province or colony on behalf of a sovereign; for example, in the 1850s a viceroy was put in charge of India on behalf of Queen Victoria.

Victoria Cross The highest British Commonwealth military honour that a soldier can win.

Index

abolition of slavery 23
Aboriginal Australians 48, 52–55
Afghanistan 61
Africa 8, 18–19, 22, 24, 25, 42, 64, 66–77
Air Force 62, 64, 65
Americas 9–21; *also see* New World
Antarctic Circle 48
apartheid 77
army 29, 30, 57, 59, 60, 62, 66, 68, 70, 71–74, 76
assassinated 38
Australia 42, 46–57, 63, 65, 81

Battle of Plassey 29
Boer War 74–75
bombs 62, 64, 65
Boston 20–21
botanists 47
Botany Bay 47, 53
Boxer Rebellion 61
British Commonwealth 76
British Empire 7
    beginning of 8–9
    benefits of 44–45, 82–83
    domination of 16
    growth of 7, 10–11, 42
    legacy of 78–81
    negative impacts of 82–83
    population of 7
    pride in 45
    size of 7, 10–11, 42
    slave trade 22–23
British Raj 34
buildings 19, 22, 45, 79

Cabot, John 9, 10
Canada 9–12, 16, 21, 42, 63, 64, 81
Caribbean 9, 16, 19, 60, 64
cartridges 30–31
ceasefire 60
Cetshwayo 70, 73
Charles II 22
Chelmsford, Lord 71, 72
China 9–11, 26–28, 61
Christians/Christianity 17, 23, 30, 47, 54, 58, 61
cities 19, 48, 57
Clarkson, Thomas 23

cod 11
Colonial Office 42–43
colonizing 10, 67
Columbus, Christopher 8, 9, 16
compensation 24–25, 59
concentration camps 74
Congress 21, 37
convicts 50–51, 56
Cook, James (Captain) 46–49, 56, 58
cotton 11, 16, 18–19, 23, 44, 68
crops 14–16, 58, 74
Cross, Ulric 62
culture 67, 78–79
customs 35, 36

democracy 81
diseases 15, 45, 48, 51, 69
disputes 16
docks 19, 44
dominion 75
Drake, Sir Francis 11
Dutch 16, 27, 28, 58, 74
dysentery 45

East India Company 13, 28–29
Easter Rising 61
Elizabeth I 10–14, 18, 22
empire-builders 6
Empire Exhibition 81
empires, definition of 6
empires, rise and fall of 7
employment 54, 65
English language 80
explorers 8–10, 67

factories 66
famine 35
Far East 8
farms 18–19, 46, 51, 53, 68, 74
fishermen 10
Flagpole War 60
flags 17, 21, 47, 57, 60
fort 14
free settlers 51, 56
French/France 16, 17, 27, 28, 42, 59

Gandhi, Mohandas 37, 38
Germany 66
Gilbert, Sir Humphrey 12

gold 11, 14, 51, 56, 66, 70
Great Rebellion (Indian Mutiny) 30–33
Great War 37

Hawkins, John 18, 22
Henry VII 8–10
Hindus 27, 30, 31, 38, 39
hunted 54
hunter-gatherers 52

immigrants/immigration 39, 78, 79
Imperial System 81
independence 21, 26, 33, 36, 39, 56–57, 59, 76–77
India 8, 10, 11, 26–39, 42, 44, 64, 79, 81
Indian Mutiny (Great Rebellion) 30–33
Ireland 61
Isandlwana 71–73

James I 14
Jamestown 14–15
'Jewel in the Crown' 34
jobs *see* employment; unemployment

Khan, Khudadad 62

Liverpool 19, 22

Magellan, Ferdinand 11
malaria 15, 67, 69
Maoris 58–60
Maroons 60
Maxim gun 68
'Mayflower' 17
merchants 18
missionaries 58
money 13, 15, 44, 65
Moscow Company 13
mother country 6
Mughals 27
Muslims 27, 30–32, 38, 39

Native Americans 13
natives 10, 12, 16, 30, 35, 47, 48, 52–55
navy 29, 46, 57, 66
New South Wales 47
New World 9, 11, 13, 15–17; *also see* Americas

New Zealand 47, 58–59, 60, 63, 65, 81
Newfoundland 9, 10, 12, 13
nomadic 52

Pacific Ocean 47–49
Parliament 57, 61, 64
'Partition of India' 36–39
Pemulwuy 53
planes 62, 65
plantations 18, 19
poor/poverty 75, 77
ports 19, 21, 28
Portugal 8–11, 67
privateers 11
punishments 19, 23, 32, 50
Puritans 17

racism 22
railways 34, 35
Raleigh, Sir Walter 12
raw materials 27, 66, 77
rebellion 29, 30–33
religions 17, 23, 27, 30–32, 36, 38, 39, 47, 54, 58, 61
Renaissance 8
resistance 53, 68
rifles 30–31, 54
road building 35
Roanoke 12–13
Roman Empire 6
Rorke's Drift 71–73
Russia 11, 13

sea routes 8; *also see* trade routes
self-government 57, 59
Sepoys 30–33
settlers 10, 12–17, 20–21, 52, 56
ships 9, 11, 12, 14, 17, 23, 28, 29, 47, 50, 51, 69
slave trade 18–19, 22–25
slave triangle 18
slaves 16, 18–19, 22–25, 60
smallpox 48
South Africa 64, 65, 77
South America 9
Spanish Empire/Spain 7–10, 16, 17, 67
Spice Islands 9–11
spices 13, 27, 28, 44
sport 77, 79, 80
starvation 15
'Stolen Generations' 54
Suez Canal 69
sugar 18–19, 23, 44

taxes 20, 24, 37
tea 20, 27, 44, 68
tobacco 11, 15, 16, 18–19, 23, 44
trade 10–12
trade routes 10, 11
trading stations 28, 29
transportation 22, 50–51
'trash gangs' 19
Treaty of Waitangi 59
tribes 12, 13, 15, 16, 47, 48, 53, 58, 59, 70–73

unemployment 45, 75
United States of America (USA) 21, 66

viceroy 33, 37
Victoria Cross 37, 62–64, 72, 73
Victoria, Queen of England 30, 32, 33, 36, 44
Virginia 10, 12–15
Virginia Company 14–15
vote 59, 81
voyages 11, 14

war 6, 7, 16, 21, 27, 29, 30–33, 37, 38, 45, 59–65, 67, 71–76
Washington, George 21
wealthy 11
West Indies 9, 22, 42, 63
Wilberforce, William 23
World War One 37, 62–63, 65, 76
World War Two 38, 62, 64–65, 76
World Wars 7, 37, 38, 45, 59, 62–65, 76

Zanzibar 67
Zulus 70–73